D1062525

FREAK CULTURE:
Life-Style and Politics

DANIEL FOSS
California Institute of the Arts

A NEW CRITICS PRESS BOOK

E. P. Dutton & Co., Inc. | *New York* | *1972*

HǪ
79ᵖ
˙F73

To Maurice R. Stein

Contents

These are the days when one asks himself the most basic questions about the movement: Is it real or transparent? Does it just concern issues, or is it a whole new life style? Could the government break it apart with concessions?

Are we creating a new Man, or are we a reflection ourselves of the bullshit we hate so much? Are we a new brotherhood, or are we just a tangle of organizations and competing egos? What will happen when we reach age 30 and 40?

I am not sure myself, and what I think often depends on how I feel when I wake up in the morning. And this is one of the differences between the white and black movements. For blacks the liberation movement is a struggle against physical and mental oppression. For whites the movement is an existential choice.

—Jerry Rubin, in *New Left Notes,* January 22, 1969

Introduction

As a vehicle of radical dissidence, the bureaucratic mass organization is now obsolete. Insofar as objective material scarcity may no longer exist, the bureaucratic mass organization's repressive structure renders it relatively incapable of formulating extreme libertarian demands based on the exploitation of historically new possibilities. Its bureaucratic structure increasingly renders it a hostage to the rapidly advancing technology of repression.

Yet the 1960s witnessed the emergence of social movements of a distinctively new type. Most significant were the movements in the black lower class and the white middle class: the principal actors were youths born since 1945. These movements responded most directly to acute contradictions, including the most important devices by which the illusion of scarcity is repressively maintained: the systematic maintenance of the black population in acute material deprivation; the continual contrivance of new needs for the purpose of sustaining and expanding the sale of consumer goods; and aggressive imperialism, materialism, and military technology.

Due to the persistence of a hallucinated culture evolved in a period of objective material scarcity, the discontented groups that were identified with the new movements sustained a dual consciousness in which, on one level, they accepted the assumption of the dominant culture that no more than peripheral reforms "within the system" were possible; while on the other level they interpreted social reality on the basis of subjective, emotional, and shared subcultural experience and felt the possibilities for drastic and far-reaching change. Large numbers of people could undergo sudden and unpredictable transitions from the first level to the second, as they simultaneously engaged in spontaneous mass disruptions, riots, and other manifestations which had their own significance (the means justify the means).

Within the discontented groups there were small *indicative minorities* whose members consistently tried to sustain the second level of consciousness (the "subjective reality") in their everyday lives. These indicative minorities maintained solidarity primarily through intensely developed subcultures rather than formal organizations. These subcultures might prominently feature such things as color consciousness and the mystical-emotional concept of "soul" (Black Nationalists) or drugs (the "freaks"). These subcultures were constantly being modified as changes were perceived in the environing society. The indicative minorities provided inspiration for and formulated the discontents of much larger groups of disaffected people.

The subjectivist ideologies current within indicative minorities tended to renounce all large bureaucratic structures as part of "the System." On this point they were in accord with administrative ideologies that represented society as a system of complexly interrelated parts. The indicative minority sought to prevent people and structures from "functioning" within "the System" by encouraging acts of disruption rather than by seeking the direct overthrow of the ruling class. A "system" relies heavily on complex planning and coordination, and is, in fact, more vulnerable to disruption and spreading chaos than it is to organized revolutionary action. Moreover, the only viable response to the technology of repression—capable of smashing any conspiratorial organization—is relatively complete unpredictability and motivations that are incomprehensible to the enemy.

The "freaks"—the white middle-class youth dropout, drug-based subculture—are represented as an indicative minority with political significance. This book will describe, interpret, and plunge the reader down in the middle of these "Kings of Eden." Let no man pass through these pages unaware that he too is a freak!

PART I

SOCIAL MOVEMENTS
AND SOCIAL STRUCTURE

The Political Logic of Bureaucratized Dissidence in the Age of Industrialization

Sociologists often slip into absurdity when dealing with nebulous and changeable processes. Our professional anxiety over assuming a proper scientific posture impels us to shun efforts to explain rationally the subtle, complex, and bewildering changes which increasingly swirl about us, especially where these involve the nastier human emotions. American sociologists are typically caught flat-footed by the appearance of new social movements; recognize their existence years too late; and then generally fail completely to foretell their ultimate directions, forms, and consequences. We now, for example, are witnessing the appearance of sociological studies in which integrationist goals are used as the basis for an index of Negro "militancy," but the ideological situation has changed tremendously since 1963 or 1964, when such studies were conceived.

It is always extremely difficult to determine the correct sociological methodology to be employed in the analysis of large-scale features and trends of a clearly unhinged society—unless, of course, one already has the inestimable advantage of hindsight. The difficulty is still further compounded if, as I believe to be the case in this society at the present time, entirely new forms of social movements, still in their early stages, have made their appearance and are, additionally, defiantly irrationalist and subjectivist in political behavior and ideology, and in which are rarely found even pretenses of coherent explanations of social reality.

The central objective of the writer should be *to figure out what the hell is going on.* This in turn should lead to a content that *must* impose itself upon form, conceptualization, and style.

I have tried to formulate a theory that rationally and systematically accounts for as many of the numerous levels on which these movements operate as I could think of. It had to include: the contradictions in the economy/polity/social structure that incline certain groups toward overt dissidence; personality types and dynamics; cultural dynamics and contradictions; changing micropolitical and macropolitical conditions and the new political logic; the historical dimension of the movements; comparisons with the past and with other societies, where possible; and discussion of emerging values and ways of life which the dissidents seek to defend or impose on institutions and on society as a whole. Not only does this make for very messy subject matter, but the movements were quite literally changing faster than I could write about them. To consider the problem from any one angle (e.g., the social-structural origins of the Reality Gap or "dual consciousness") reveals a certain set of causal interrelationships. While I was in the midst of trying to understand and then systematically describe social crises, another series of crises would break out and the newspapers would be full of clichés to the effect that no matter what the end result would be, X (a city, a university, an entire country) "would never be quite the same again." Ideologues among the dissidents would, in their post facto analysis, convert what had hitherto been vaguely perceived implications into overt formulations and then into folk sayings, as when the New Left, in the months following Columbia and Chicago, endlessly reiterated the slogan "Confrontation *is* education."

Meanwhile, with history unfolding all of the time, the movements changed internally so that the vision seemed to be analogous to turning a kaleidoscope; you can't look at the same pattern twice.

Under these conditions, my original objective of using a "methodology" appropriate to the analysis of an "unhinged society" somehow got lost. What I seemed actually to have used, reflecting the messiness of the social reality I was trying to deal with, is more like "messodology"; I was determined that any theory of social movements in the 1960s had to account systematically for all the strange evanescent-looking phenomena, weird events, "senseless violence," "irresponsible extremism," "Rebels without a Program," "Alienated Youth," and "Generation Gaps" that had come to my attention in the two movements I was most especially interested in. A point has been reached where it is better to be completely wrong than to be insufficiently right.

Out of these "messodology" a typology of social movements evolved that included such criteria as: the social classes involved in the movement; size and sophistication of organizational forms emerging at various stages of the movement, as well as the political and economic strategies and tactics employed at these stages; relations of enmity or alliance with other social categories, groups and classes; and degrees of correspondence between the various kinds of consciousness and ideology current within the movement and the objective interests of the social class, group, or category in question. Also, I classified social movements according to their "intensity," or, in other words, the political stakes involved at the peak of the movement. (Some social movements subside after registering mild protests, while others go on to bring about major revisions of public policy as desired by the interest groups involved in them, while still others topple regimes or even bring about complete social revolutions.)

This typology was largely based on a generalized image of the capitalist societies of Europe and the United States during the age of industrialization and immediately thereafter. Typically, one would find at the top of the social structure a relatively small class of industrialists, financiers, and other owners, who were gradually acquiring more and more concentrated control over the economy as the large bureaucratic corporation became the dominant form of economic institution. A large and mostly undifferentiated and unskilled class of factory operatives, miners, and other blue-collar employees was being assembled to work under hierarchically regimented conditions in increasingly large factories (dominated by assembly-line production) and other large work establishments. Between these two classes lay the "middle class," which at this time was smaller everywhere than the industrial working class, though steadily growing. This middle class was, of course, itself very complexly stratefied and lacking clearly defined limits at the upper end (owners of enterprises too small to be considered "big business"; corporate managers and salaried specialists; high career state officials; most "free" professionals) or at the lower end (clerical and semiprofessional workers; shopkeepers; salesmen, etc.). In addition, each country had a relatively backward agricultural sector with problems of its own.

Social movements are marked by sudden increases in the proportions of the total number of people in the social categories upon which such movements are based who are thinking and acting politically (in the broadest sense of this word); and also by the new intensity with which they so think and act. People do things which they have never done before and which "simply aren't done." Given the course of capitalist industrial development and the growth of the state bureaucracies, it was inevitable that the disaffected would draw the conclusion that power was increasingly in the hands of those who commanded centralized, complex, hierarchical, disciplined, and efficient organizations. Marxism is not necessary to arrive at such a conclusion; Marxist doctrine can, however, give it intellectual coherence and historical relevance.

For decades, therefore, social movements in both Europe and the United States came to their close with the development of larger, more centralized, disciplined, efficient, and complex interest-group organizations (or counterorganizations) than had been present at earlier stages of these movements. The political scene became littered with all kinds of special-interest, mass-membership organizations: trade unions, farmers' unions, cooperative societies, employers' associations, chambers of commerce, political parties of all hues, veterans' groups, tribal, linguistic, and religious protective associations, professional associations, "leagues" for this and "societies" against that.

Wherever reasonable credible parliamentary regimes existed (and even where parliaments labored under gross and obvious limitations, as in Imperial Germany), the assumption that the road to major reform, social justice, and perhaps even revolution lay in the disciplined and rationally informed manipulation of the power of numbers and the power of the vote appeared highly plausible to activist elements among the new industrial working classes. Social movements based on this class would therefore be marked, in addition to the sudden spread of trade unionism, by dramatically increased interest in obtaining favorable legislation in such areas as the suppression of repressive state practices and policy ("conspiracy" laws; injunctions) that inhibited the establishment, freedom of action, and institutional security of trade unions; social insurance programs; inspection; constitutional and electoral reform; and general civil liberties. Mass political parties thus developed alongside or in structural association with the inclusive mass unions themselves.

Social movements based on the industrial proletariat inevitably imitated or reflected the existence of the centralized bureaucratic state and the development of centralizing, increasingly bureaucratized, increasingly cartelized industrial capitalism. The specialized role of the "organizer"—labeled as such—appeared (in Germany during the 1890s) as a full-time, paid staff position. Other mass-organization staff specialties included financial administration (fund-raising and dues collection), journalism, legal services, economic and statistical research, and theoretical elaboration of Marxist ideology. Such developments were, in part, conditioned by mass literacy and the new technology of mass communications, and also themselves provided the resources for access to and exploitation of the mass media. The new organizational forms were also conditioned by the spread of the mass-production factory technology, with its concentrated assemblages of unskilled and semiskilled laborers, which offered the only realistic means of producing a stable institutional impact upon that system. The bureaucratized unions and parties could also provide an apparently impressive accumulation of resources for their own protection in the form of strike funds; a network of journals, periodicals, and other agencies of mass communication; propaganda and internal education; organized membership in the millions; and extensive representation in parliamentary bodies. In Germany, by the time of World War I, all this had the semblance of a "state within a state." This edifice was, however, less impressive in terms of actual power than its adherents believed, or some of its opponents feared.

The mass organizations that confronted the European centralized bureaucratic states (and, in most cases, their closely allied churches), centralized and bureaucratized industrial capitalism,

and other mass organizations sought, in effect, to standardize political consciousness. The member's interpretation of social reality
was to be treated as an assembly-line product, with uniform and
interchangeable parts. It became understood that mass-membership
political parties, especially, would uphold some sort of doctrine or
ideology which at least pretended to a comprehensive explanation
of social reality (Marxism, Liberalism, political Catholicism, Nationalism, etc.). Since Marxists, in particular, believed themselves
to be custodians of a "scientific" social theory, it was not sufficient
for members of Marxist mass organizations merely to pay dues and
participate in organized activities; constant efforts had to be made
to "raise the level of consciousness" of the membership, to inculcate
"objective class consciousness," to eliminate "subjectivism" and
"irrationalism," and to nullify the impact of the "bourgeois" mass
media. During the most intense phases of social movements based
on the industrial working classes, the "ultimate" missions of the
socialist mass organizations as the "gravediggers of capitalism"
and the forerunners of a new social order were commonly featured
in their propaganda and rhetoric. As these movements subsided,
however, it would become apparent that the *de facto* goals of
socialist trade unions were the Welfare State and immediate small
improvements in living standards; leaders of socialist parties were
becoming visibly assimilated into the "bourgeois" political system.

A series of crises, beginning in 1914, revealed the fundamental
weakness of the great mass working-class organizations of Europe,
despite their appearance of imposing strength: although having a
long tradition of internationalism and pacifism, they could do absolutely nothing to arrest the drift into World War I; they then enthusiastically and almost universally supported the war efforts of
their respective countries—almost until the end of the war. In the
great Europe-wide (if not worldwide) social crisis following the
war, they proved singularly incapable of responding to pressures
from below; activist and dissident minorities in most countries (including the United States, where a parody of the European experience took place) seceded to form communist parties and unions
which coupled a repudiation of "reformism" and "revisionism"
with an ever more complete insistence on total centralized bureaucratic control, uniformity, and rigid discipline—the Party itself was
conceived as a piece of machinery.

The European working-class mass organizations later failed totally to develop realistic and effective long-range political strategies for dealing with either the Depression or the threat of fascism.

While the United States was, throughout most of this same period, the most advanced nation, both in terms of its technology and its techniques of economic organization, it has experienced the development of mass-membership, comprehensive "industrial" unions only in the recent past (the labor movement of the 1930s), while the European-type mass-membership, explicitly ideological political party has not taken root at all. A variety of explanations has been offered by historians to account for the failure of American labor movements to develop along more "European" lines: the existence of a monolithically bourgeois culture (i.e., since feudal institutions never really existed here, it was not necessary for capitalism to emerge through the destruction of a much older social order; consequently, Americans could not derive from their own history the idea of the transitoriness of class systems); a historic labor shortage and, consequently, a relatively high standard of living even during the most acute traumas of industrialization; the arrival, during the most critical periods of the industrialization process, of a mass of European expeasants, divided and burdened by language barriers, which could easily be transformed into a servile and helpless industrial proletariat; persistence of large areas of opportunity for small business, despite extensive concentration of the economy into large corporate structures; the "frontier" as a safety valve; the absence until relatively recent times of a powerful, centralized, bureaucratic state; the tradition, until recently, of the state as serving primarily as a passive source of subsidies rather than as an active intervener in the economy and a protector of the weak from the worst social abuses; the vulnerable and exposed position of incipient labor movements in the face of uncontrolled private violence, spasmodic, populistic "red scares" (as in 1886, 1894, 1919, and 1947–1954), and "tribal" (anti-Irish, anti-Negro, etc.) violence; a cultural tradition of anarchic individual assertiveness associated with universality of the ownership of firearms, which inhibited the conceptualization of social conflict and, consequently, the idea of organization.

In any case, social movements of the type which gave rise to mass organizations of the industrial working class are technologically, sociologically, politically, and culturally obsolete in what is sometimes called "postindustrial" (or "postmodern") society. The social movements of the 1960s cannot be characterized, even for the short term, in the simpleminded rhetoric of an opposition between the forces of "progress/change/the future/movement" and the forces of "reaction/status quo/the past/order." The opposition is between forces seeking antithetical systems of institutionalized change. Neither side would be possible or conceivable without widespread use of advanced technology and a diffusion through society of a high material standard of living. On the Right are ranged the holders of power—the capitalists, technocrats, and their allies and subordinates—the logic of whose interests leads them to seek to bring into existence the "technetron": a totally planned and smoothly functioning society in which the behavior of people proceeds from the necessities of the organized whole. On the Left are found forces whose interests logically lead them to seek to bring into existence the "universal mess"; a society in which people do whatever they want to do and are rewarded primarily by the doing of it. Both tendencies can coexist within this society and even among millions of individuals (whence the Reality Gap) for a length of time that is not easily, if at all, predictable. But after May 1968 in France, I became convinced that the Apocalypse could happen—complete with people painting each other in the streets. And I am not talking about a "revolution" with Hollywood peasants storming a Winter Palace. It is possible to envision something which either will not happen at all or in which, should it happen, the existing political regime will not be "overthrown" so much as it will get lost in the shuffle.

In other words, while the mass-membership organizations of the industrial proletariat, farmers, the middle classes (whether in their liberal-reformist or conservative-reactionary guises), "tribal" or ethnic groups, and special-interest groups will doubtless continue to exist for a long time, the social movements of the future will not be marked primarily (or even at all) by the rapid growth of such organizations. The new social movements will instead be marked primarily by extreme informality and spontaneity of collective behavior; episodic frenzy; disruption of bureaucratic organizations by means of confronting them with unpredictable and unprecedented behavior; the absence of identifiable leadership and chains of command; the rapid rise and even more rapid decline of oppositional anticultures; and an intense ideological insistence on subjective experience.

Before going further into the problem of the special characteristics of emerging social movements, it will be necessary to discuss the structure of the emerging American society, its contradictions, and its sources of revolt.

CHAPTER 2

The Technological Obsolescence of Bureaucratized Dissidence Under Conditions of Advanced Industrial Capitalism

John K. Galbraith, in his recent book *The New Industrial State* (1967), presents a reasonably fair picture of the principal features of the economic and social organization of this society—at least with respect to the domestic functioning of the major organized institutions of the society. It can, of course, be argued that the impact of these institutions—corporations and federal government—upon other societies constitutes a major structural feature of the system which, additionally, might be crucial in systematically, if indirectly, generating domestic revolt as well as potential instability of consumer demand. His book is one of the few specimens of intelligent comprehensive "macrosociological" thought to appear in recent years.

Galbraith, with a consistent materialism commendable in an American social theorist, discerns as the most basic force acting to transform the structure of this society the ever-increasing introduction of more sophisticated and costly technologies into the processes of industrial production. Control over industrial production was, of course, concentrated decades ago in the heads of a few hundred large, bureaucratic corporations formed originally for purposes of maximizing profits, since this form of organization conferred economies of scale, suppression of price competition, greater bargaining power vis-à-vis external sources of capital, ability to overawe and even terrorize the labor force, direct control over elected and appointed public officials, and opportunity for stock watering and other nonrespectable financial manipulations. But the era of the 1920s, perhaps even the era of the 1940s, is, by comparison with the present, a long-vanished, simple, almost pastoral age. Since those long-lost days, Galbraith holds, the requirements of the latest technologies have compelled modifications in the internal organization and functioning of industrial corporations. (At least among the ever smaller number of ever more enormous units able to introduce the most advanced technologies—the process of concentration continues unabated.)

Galbraith first notes that the corporation must, as a matter of course, engage in long-range planning. Highly intricate and expensive capital equipment, large aggregations of skilled manpower, and vast organizational resources are tied up for periods of years in conceiving, developing, and analyzing the potential market for the product; for designing, manufacturing, and finally selling it. And this product must, in turn, be accepted as up-to-date at the time it is put on sale. Such a huge investment of capital and skills, committed for such a long period, can be justified only if the risk of failure is minimized. Sources of interference, disruption, and uncertainty must be as nearly as possible eliminated.

Such a corporation is so large and secure that it rarely loses money. It therefore generally has a stable and predictable source of investment capital; additionally, it is secure from the prying and potentially disruptive activities of financial institutions, as well as from its own stockholders. Supplies of crucial, skilled, and highly educated personnel are secured in advance. General levels of prices and wages are stabilized through state policy, while more specific wage and price costs are held steady by means of long-term contracts with trade unions and suppliers. Selling prices of products are administratively determined on the assumption that consumer demand is predictable well in advance. This latter assumption is fulfilled through the systematic use of the mass media not only to stimulate demand for existing products, but to create needs for products still under development. The most onerous and risky research-and-development costs are borne by the state; but the corporation is normally assured of immunity from state interference in its internal operations.

Galbraith's second great preoccupation is with the rise of a large and rapidly growing class of experts—scientists, engineers, technicians, designers, motivational researchers, market analysts, sales and promotion specialists, personnel-placement psychologists, and numerous other categories of specialists—who are indispensable to the continued development and efficient utilization of the new (and always newer) technology. Such people, whose skills and talents gain them important posts in the corporate organizational structure—increasingly even at top management levels—constitute, in Galbraith's view, a large and potent interest group in any "mature" corporation, where they gradually if not imperceptibly acquire power at the expense of the old entrepreneur-financier-lawyer-bureaucrat types of managements. This new ruling elite and the logical consequence of the new technology are accorded by Galbraith the name "technostructure." The most basic defining characteristic of the "technostructure" is the specialized scientific education, training, and expertise of its members. It is actually a subclass, since in its upper reaches, at least, it is not sharply distinguishable from older entrepreneurial and managerial groups. Such a process of ruling-class assimilation and reconsolidation, not always painless, might be considered vaguely parallel to that by which eighteenth- and nineteenth-century European entrepreneur-industrialists acquired titles of nobility and other conections with the traditional landed governing class.

The technostructure, according to Galbraith (Chapter VI), normally functions within the corporation as a hierarchical series of "committees"—including formal continuing bodies, *ad hoc* groupings necessitated by immediate problems, and informal and unrecognized associational cliques—which pool and share information to achieve shared objectives. Decisions emerging from such bodies cannot normally be overruled at higher echelons, since they are based on expert knowledge; moreover, the responsibility is shared among the members of the group. The basic decision-making processes of the corporation, then, come to be centered in these committees of the technostructure.

Galbraith rightly points out that this model of organizational behavior, with its emphasis on group decision-making as well as lateral contact within the organization cutting across formal vertical chains of command, differs radically from the conventional image of bureaucratic organization, where power is concentrated at the "pinnacle"; responsibility and information move up a clearly defined chain of command; and orders move down just as surely. It is perhaps not irrelevant that Max Weber's ideal-type theory of bureaucracy, upon which many of the more intellectualized versions of this conventional imagery are ultimately based, was formulated in a Germany undergoing rapid industrialization and seared by manifestly intense class hatred. Weber's ideal-type bureaucrat, while certified by competitive examination as a specialist, was hardly an innovator. His activities were standardized and routinized, after the fashion of the assembly line; he was bound by rules, regulations, and precedents. He functioned within a carefully ordered and graded hierarchy in which promotion was methodical and based on performance "by the book." His duties normally emphasized transactions up and down the chain of command, and would have presented few opportunities for group decision-making in committees constituted laterally across the organizational pyramid. The ideal-type Weberian bureaucrat, routinized as his post was supposed to have been, by definition did not make policy; he supposedly carried it out in an impartial and impersonal fashion without letting his subjective predispositions obtrude. Policy-making was the prerogative of "generalists" at the top. The latter, in Weber's Germany, would, of course, typically turn out to be Junkers or plutocratic cartel dynasts and their managerial tools. Weber maintained that armies tended most nearly to exemplify ideal-typical bureaucratic organizations.

Weber's model of bureaucracy plainly did not represent the most efficient possible use of specialist personnel and technical expertise. Yet, given the extensive authoritarianism and militarism of Imperial Germany, we can accept the proposition that Weber—an acute observer and a man of encyclopedic knowledge—realistically reflected organizational realities, at least as they prevailed in Germany. Given the relatively simple technology and relatively slow rate of technological change, compared with conditions prevailing today, the authoritarian-hierarchical model would, however, appear as an amazingly efficient, if not the most efficient possible, form of organization. Also, in that (by our standards) relatively uncomplicated social and technological environment, as it persisted until World War I, there was no great cultural strain for members of the German middle class to fill bureaucratic posts in large organizations while adhering to such traditional virtues and attitudes as duty and loyalty to Fatherland, Kaiser, state, employer, organizational superior, etc., family reputation, prudence, thrift, servility to landed and industrial barons, contempt for the proletariat, and self-restraint. Culturally speaking, such people would have been ready-formed interchangeable parts and tools, even if well educated and, in many cases, academics and scientists with advanced degrees. The bureaucrats, unsurprisingly therefore, formed a nearly solid instrument of the ruling classes in the suppression of the turbulence of the lower classes.

The Weberian model of bureaucracy, in short, described a form of organization directed substantially toward the repressive reinforcement of the existing class system during a very critical period in the social history of industrialization, as well as toward its manifest objective of technical efficiency. It is not, however, the complex technology *alone* that makes for the growing power of the experts; rather, this technology is introduced in a social structure marked by full industrialization, stable and gradually rising mass-consumption affluence, a consolidated and highly planned economy whose central institutions are not subject to serious challenge, and a condition of long term class *détente* between labor and management. Since the social-control functions of large bureaucratic organizations are not continually being called upon (because of ongoing and intense conflict across the line dividing blue- and white-collar employees), the rising pressures requiring the most efficient possible utilization of expert personnel are permitted to operate without concerted resistance being offered. A new kind of organization subculture, dominated by the experts' need to identify with the organization and with each other, gradually develops.

In time, scientists, technicians, engineers, all other experts and intellectuals and then, after a while, everyone else in the society finds it increasingly impossible to function efficiently and in comfort under conditions of hierarchical-authoritarian regimentation.

We are all familiar with the model of change within the bureaucratic corporation that was presented in the early 1950s by William H. Whyte, Jr., in *The Organization Man*. Largely impressionistically, Whyte first described what he felt to have been the prevailing organizational subculture at the time of his youth, which he called the "Protestant Ethic." In this type of subculture, organizational superiors were themselves often lacking in formal higher education, but prided themselves on their ultrapragmatism and their single-minded ferocity in the pursuit of profit as well as personal wealth and power. They had near-absolute hierarchical authority over their subordinates, whom they treated with ruthlessness, relating individual achievement solely to the profits of the enterprise. The subordinates, in turn, were encouraged to engage in a Darwinian rivalry among themselves, so that only those who excelled in personal aggressiveness, initiative, and lust for gain were deemed fit for the very few positions in the upper reaches of the hierarchy. The enterprise was assumed, perhaps unjustifiably, to be operating within a competitive market situation, with the maximization of profit being understood as vital to the survival of the firm, if not almost the sole reason for its existence. Moreover, the executives of that day, if not exactly conscious of class barriers, were at least exceedingly aware of the gulf between the few who succeeded and the masses of failures.

To this Whyte contrasted the "Social Ethic," which he thought to be the typical corporate subculture of the early 1950s. Assertion of hierarchical authority was muted or disguised; younger executives craved a sort of glad-handing conformist camaraderie with their peers; the appearance of rivalry for advancement was suppressed; individuals identified themselves, their interests, and their life patterns with the organization and its goals; and young men yearned for personal security within the organization above all else. Those molded in this subculture assumed that their careers would take the form of a slow, mechanical, "escalator"-like rise; it was to be anticipated that the steady growth of the organization would continue to provide sufficient room at the top. This, however, required the still more implicit assumption that the organization was sufficiently immune from the unpredictable effects of market forces so that it could provide long-term security for itself as well as for its officials throughout their careers. By the 1950s, the spread of mass-consumption affluence had led to widely remarked cultural traits of organization people: anxieties over status and personal image, and sophistication in distinguishing minute status differentials. Finally, the onset of the new technology and the age of Big Research appeared to be handled in a manner congruent with the pattern as a whole: the corporations sought out and stockpiled large numbers of scientists, engineers, and other technical personnel, but took care to shun and repel potential employees afflicted with genius and other organizationally disruptive personality characteristics.

The technostructure elite, as Galbraith describes it, appears to have consolidated itself at a time when corporate subcultures, for complex reasons, were marked by declining authoritarianism. The growing power of the technostructure, in turn, further modified these subcultures—which in the early 1950s were still sufficiently fluid and novel to appear to observers such as Whyte as a decadent deterioration of the American tradition—in the direction of the increased valuation of technical expertise, esoteric knowledge, and precise coordinated planning. It would appear that genius, creativity, and eccentricities of personality among technical personnel are at least no longer feared, and some corporations now de-emphasize team playing and security in their recruiting efforts, emphasizing instead their scope for individual creativity, intellectual challenge on the frontiers of science, and relevance to contemporary social issues. (Bell Telephone Laboratories now includes the lyrics of a Bob Dylan song in its campus recruiting advertisements.)

Galbraith argues, as has already been said, that the power of the technostructure rests upon its presumptive control over the complex new technologies in modern industry. Among the most important of these technologies are those of electronic communications, including most crucially the mass media and advanced techniques of information gathering, processing, storage, and retrieval. The mass media, as Galbraith so aptly points out, make possible the rational and predictable management of demand and the systematic creations of new needs. This inescapably imparts to consumption a repressive and enforced dimension, and hence constitutes a potential object of any revolt which might be generated within the system.

That this has been true of the new social movements of the 1960s is obvious: the various dissident middle-class youth cultures feature as prominent theses the ostentatious rejection of mass-produced consumer durables in favor of chemical, emotional, or political gratifications, which are seen as offering liberation from the compulsive and alienated treadmill of consumption. Most visible to the general public has been the hippie practice of wearing filthy odds and ends, blankets, flags, Boer War uniforms, and other objects normally inconceivable as clothing. Meanwhile, at the bottom of the social scale, it appears that repressive consumption has its consequence in the forcible acquisition by masses of people of what is offered for sale. It is clear that a major component of the emotional fuel driving the black ghetto masses to insurrection derives from their being subject to incessant bombardment by the media, especially television, with injunctions to consume the impedimenta and accouterments of white middle-class life. This pressure is exerted not exclusively nor even primarily through advertising, but rather by means of the general impact of the program content of the mass media as a whole, since this content is overwhelmingly concerned with a vapid presentation of white middle-class life. The black audience is therefore both frustrated by the inaccessibility of the white middle-class standard of living and tempted into assuming an appalling burden of installment debt, involving the payment of several times the standard price for the goods—out of welfare or other inadequate income. All this contributes to the fury with which stores are sacked and burned during ghetto rebellions: the desire for ownership is combined with the impulse to destroy the system of repressive consumption and the local institutions identified with it. We will return to this problem when considering the political implications of the impact of television upon culture.

The new technologies of information gathering and manipulation are vital to the technostructure and to industry as a whole, since they make possible the long-range planning and instantaneous feedback-correction without which raw materials, parts, machines, people, and money cannot be brought together as required. Planning for distant goals must be elaborate; control over every step between the formulation of the plan and the arrival at the goal must be as precise as the sophistication of the technology and the power of the organization permit. Otherwise there is the possibility of disaster or fantastic waste. An airline, for example, must estimate passenger volume years in advance by feeding the necessary demographic, economic, and sociological data into the computer; only in this way is it able to place orders for aircraft still in the design or prototype stage, lobby for the construction of airports at small but rapidly growing cities, and acquire franchises for runs that will become lucrative only in the future. But it must also know, again with help from the computers, the precise number of reservations at any moment for each flight, as well as the exact location at each instant of every aircraft. The passenger, of course, is expected to have almost unconscious confidence in the certainty of this precision organization functioning perfectly; he is told to relax and enjoy the "friendly skies."

It is no secret that the electronic technologies of precise coordination have generalized themselves far beyond the industrial system and the "private" corporation; governmental, quasi-governmental, educational, religious, and other kinds of organizations also have their data-processing equipment to plan ahead, keep track, snoop, allocate, channel, and select. Naturally, prestige considerations enter into some decisions to computerize, since he who has not even one third-generation computer to call his own is a self-confessed small-time operator. More importantly, of course, the incessant rise in the sheer volume of data and the need to harmonize the system of data output in one large organization with the data input requirements of another functionally related large organization make inevitable the spread of this technology to all organizations of any size. The accurate prediction and detailed control (statistically speaking, at least) of the behavior of people at all levels of the society will therefore become increasingly a matter of delicate precision. With the growing, complex interdependence of all organizations (and of their data-processing systems, via Data-Phone), a costly error made by one organization (or a major disruption suffered by it) would require elaborate and extremely rapid readjustments by many others. Obviously, we can expect more and more refined and intricate data collection and analysis, by and within large organizations, of the most minute social variables, relevant or not. Obviously, too, we can expect data on individuals—whether authorized and legally collected or not—to be centrally stored and ceaselessly analyzed in "data banks," including some which are kept secret for "security" purposes, while others are acknowledged to the public.

Without question, such a situation—with respect to its present state or to its fuller emergence in the future—drastically undermines the political rationality of the mass-membership bureaucratic organization as the "traditional" form of dissidence and resistance to the industrial establishment. It is becoming increasingly impossible for bureaucratically organized dissidents to compete with their opponents in ability to plan rationally in terms of their own interests; in access to vital data and information on policy; in speed and thoroughness of reaction; in speed of communication; in organizational resources; and in precise and coordinated control over the activities of large numbers of people.

Consider, for example, what happens to the tactic of the mass demonstration, a device characteristic of social movements of the industrial era. The operating rationale is that mass organizations can, through demonstrations, directly impress the authorities with the size, discipline, and militancy of their followings. The mass demonstration is almost impossible without a great deal of advance planning, coordination, logistics, and low-level organizational legwork. In a situation where the disproportion between the resources available to the authorities and those available to the mass organizations is not as great as it now is in this society, the desired impression could perhaps be made. But the actual irrelevance of such a demonstration under contemporary conditions is dramatically illustrated in the account by a former Defense Department official of the antiwar demonstration held in Washington, D.C., October 21–22, 1967, which ended with a planned "confrontation" on the steps of the Pentagon:

> My awareness of the extent to which the demonstration was controlled by the Pentagon stems from my thorough familiarity with the Pentagon's plans—and the demonstrators'—well before the demonstration. I was, at the time, stationed at the Pentagon in a highly placed intelligence-and-security unit. Our job, essentially, was to observe, report and coordinate information; we had been planning for the demonstration since August, and at Thanksgiving we were still collating reports of arrests. I read several thousand pages of government reports, I knew what was expected of us and of the protesters, and I was appalled to see how neatly the government had the peace movement pegged. . . .
>
> The Pentagon not only knew what moves were being planned against it; it also displayed consummate virtuosity in handling both the protection of the building and the manipulation of news. . . .
>
> Intelligence reported that a demonstration would take place. The Pentagon started its overall planning, which became more

specific as more EEI [Essential Elements of Information] came in. Basically, the Pentagon found out the date of the demonstration and the approximate number of participants, together with their organizational affiliations, leaders and means of transportation.

This estimate was considerably more accurate than the estimate of the sponsors of the march, since it was based on chats with the operators of nearly every bus company in the United States, visits to the "ride to Washington" bulletin boards of colleges and other gathering places, and religious attendance at meetings of the participating groups.

Although the Department of Defense likes publicly to minimize the danger, and especially to provide low estimates of the number of demonstrators, privately they put some of their best planners and security officers on the job. The planners dreamed; they accepted the mundane and the fantastic. Beginning with a list of every possible move the marchers could make, they outlined the steps required to restore the status quo (which is in all cases what the Army will try to do), and they determined the logistics requirements: how many men, for how long, which units, what equipment.

In Vietnam, this procedure has failed; on the Pentagon lawn it worked perfectly. The Army had the marchers' moves planned for weeks ahead and, because of the massive coordination of its intelligence and communications nets, knew better than any single demonstrating group the plans of every group of participants, from the Michigan busloads to the East Village hippies. The minor details, such as who would try to break in and who would be arrested, were left up to the demonstrators.

We had the orders, neatly mimeographed: anyone setting himself on fire was to be extinguished with blankets. At convenient locations barely out of sight, blankets were ready. Conferences with firefighting authorities revealed that CO_2 fire extinguishers freeze the victim, and soda-acid types damage the skin. Plain water turns the victim into a boiled frankfurter. . . .[1]

The October 1967 demonstration was as illustrative of the emergence of new political techniques as it was of the obsolescence of old ones; it was an instance of new content being forced into an inappropriate antique form.

In listing the forces precipitating the development of the subjective consciousness characteristic of the new social movements, consideration must be given to the information-gathering activities of large and complex organizations. Under this very general heading we are considering: first, the ever-broadening scope and ever-increasing volume of data on the behavior of individuals that are gathered and processed, in a rather routine and neutral fashion, by corporations, financial institutions, educational institutions, and the state, in their efforts to maximize the efficiency of their normal and increasingly precision-coordinated activities; second (and not entirely separate and distinct from the first), the clandestine activities identified principally but not exclusively with the state, such as infiltration, surveillance, and "bugging," which are rationalized as being essential for purposes of insuring "national security" against alleged subversion by hostile states, as well as "internal security" and "law and order" against alleged threats to the social order represented by disaffected groups and individuals. Logically, we must also consider the impact upon consciousness, especially among youth, of the awareness of the existence, in the activities of large organizations, of "planning," "policy-" and "decision-making," and executive action which are either secret or deliberately concealed and disguised, while based in part on the elaborately detailed available information on individual behavior.

Weber identified the keeping of records and files as one of the major defining characteristics of the ideal-typical bureaucracy; no large and complex organization could seemingly survive without extensive storage of documents. The accumulation of records is, of course, vastly facilitated by electronic technologies. With the growing importance of high-speed, precision-coordinated operations, large organizations have expedited their activities by putting enormous quantities of data (on the physical characteristics, personalities, financial status, and achievements of individuals) on cards and tape. Obviously, very little of this (excepting, of course, the intentions of police forces and the Federal Bureau of Investigation) has been consciously planned for political purposes—as a means of maintaining or increasing social control. More commonly, the motive is improvement of the organization's control over, and otherwise its ability to predict change in, its own immediate environment. The data are used in predicting and analyzing consumer behavior and "public opinion," in actuarial analysis, in personnel practices, in formulating "profiles" of entering freshmen classes and alumni, in assessing credit risks, granting draft deferments, checking tax returns, approving driver's license applications, examining medical case histories, and so on. It is difficult to determine that any *particular* instance of expanded data collection, instituted for the purpose of increased efficiency or lowered costs, nevertheless represents—taken by itself—an intolerable encroachment upon the private domain of the individual.

Accordingly, we have on file by the millions, and in various places, compilations of birthmarks, fingerprints, case histories, arrest records, personality-test results, achievement- and aptitude-test scores, academic performance records from grade school to graduate school (together with comments and evaluations by teachers, advisers, etc.), financial statements, bank balances, hotel registrations, long-distance telephone calls, airline tickets, records of consumer purchases, paid and unpaid parking tickets, credit ratings, job performance evaluations, security and loyalty checks (by "private" employers and self-constituted anticommunist crusaders, as well as by the state), and much more.

The quantity of all these data, which are instantaneously retrievable and instantaneously exchangeable among organizations and divisions of organizations, is certainly growing. It could grow much faster with the development of faster computers with more miniaturized storage. The spreading use of credit cards for small consumer purchases vastly increases the theoretical possibilities of individuals leaving permanent documentary traces of even their pettiest movements.

The logical culmination of such current processes would be the so-called "National Data Bank," where all this data would be stored and therefore instantaneously available for processing when required by the authorities. (For example, the Selective Service System could have a weekly or even daily report on the precise current employment status of all occupationally deferred registrants.) A crude initial version of this system has already been proposed. However, given the theoretical possibilities of the "Dataphone," it is not really necessary for all the data to be physically stored on one master set of tapes. (Selective Service could place daily calls to Social Security or Internal Revenue and check its II-A tapes against the constant flow of information on terminations of employment. Then it could check with the FBI computer to get the latest information on persons rumored to have mentioned something about possibly fleeing the country.) All this might take place in the interests of "efficiency" and "economy."

Already exchanges of information and lists of names (these lists being marketable commodities) of donors, signers, and consumers, among even relatively small organizations are transforming the purchase of consumer durables into something other than "private" transactions between dealer and customer (ignoring, for the moment, the state agencies that register the article and collect sales and excise taxes). To cite a trivial example, in 1967 I bought a used car in Syracuse, New York. In short order I received a brochure from St. Paul, Minnesota, advertising the wares of a slipcover manufacturer, and at least one solicitation for some oil-company credit-card plan.

One of the aspects of efficiency conferred by the accumulation of detailed data on the behavior and other characteristics of individuals is that pertaining to the "use," "allocation," "channeling," and, generally speaking, the coordination of large masses of "personnel." People are chosen, distributed, admitted, transferred, promoted, reorganized, and generally manipulated in a pattern believed by experts to be most efficient in achieving the objectives of the technostructure and such other elite groups with which it shares power in the organization in question. This increasingly implies the use of highly sophisticated administrative techniques, which are the domain of industrial psychologists, industrial sociologists, personality testers, guidance counselors, and "community–relations," "human–relations," and "conflict–resolution" specialists, as well as those assistant deans of students who make a point of interlarding their speech with the latest argot of student-protest subcultures. The sophisticated manipulation of people within organizations is not the product of some malign conspiracy to impose totalitarian domination; even when the object of administrators is the suppression of conflict, this is seen in terms of avoiding "trouble" or "raising morale." Brutal and heavy-handed authoritarianism of the Pinkerton and Company goon variety is, indeed, increasingly obsolescent; dissidents are, instead, confronted by baffling evasiveness, flattery, ad hoc committees, special study groups, joint advisory boards, periodic informal administrator-subordinate conferences at mountain lake retreats, and numerous social functions and picnics intended to establish a pseudo-community or pseudo-familial atmosphere.

The sophisticated "processing" of "personnel" within large organizations becomes linked to the manipulation of people in the aggregate by means of advertising and the mass culture. Business firms whose executives are most vociferous in extolling the traditional bourgeois virtues will, in the name of the bourgeois ideal of efficiency, institute personality tests in the selection of new employees (especially salesmen and other nonmanual personnel having extensive contact with the public), as well as in the upgrading of existing ones ("human resources development"). Generally speaking, the psychological-testing experts will bias their instruments to the advantage of products of the mass culture. Similarly, the extensive collection of data on educational achievement facilitates the spread of educational criteria in hiring practices —often into situations where they are irrelevant, as in hiring for unskilled manual jobs where, say, a high-school diploma is of no conceivable significance in actually performing the work involved. In turn, the educational system responds by administering aptitude tests to children at ever earlier ages. All this stimulates the obsession with formal educational achievement that is one of the distinguishing features of the mass culture, insofar as this achievement is perceived as guaranteeing "success." Meanwhile, groups which are outside the mass culture (though constantly exposed to and bombarded by it), such as the black lower class, find their children stigmatized at early ages as inferior. The children themselves are sensitive to this treatment, since even third graders distinguish between "smart" and "stupid" classes despite the authorities' efforts at terminological disguise. The school staffs regard the children as inferior and treat them accordingly. Demoralized and infuriated by this treatment, youths will flee the schools as soon as possible and thereby will be condemned to marginal employment in the backwaters of the economy.

The interrelation of the dossier society with the mass culture produces a juxtaposition of the reality of the manipulated, dependent person with the still universally accepted bourgeois cultural ideal of the autonomous, self-reliant, unique individual. The urge to escape from this contradiction appears to be an important element in the recent recrudescence of the romantic-reactionary Right, as personified by Barry Goldwater and, in a much more modernized form, by Ronald Reagan and his "Creative Society" regime in California. Reagan is presented as the perfect embodiment of the mass culture: well meaning, undistinguished, sincere, bland, contented, stable, domesticated, ambitious but not pushy; his public image blends into his "good guy" roles on television and in films; his bumbling in public is held to contrast favorably with the supposedly devious ways of politicians and bureaucrats. The Reagan people seek to combine the two major large, nondissenting classes of the "industrial system," the organizational middle class and the unionized skilled proletariat, against the two obviously dissenting classes, the black (and Latin) lower class and the academic middle class (or, in Galbraith's terminology, the "Educational and Scientific Estate") with its student and hippie vanguard. The nondissenting classes are invited to combine at their point of common material interest—as payers of property taxes on their suburban and suburbanlike homes. The political "program" is (apart from the imposition of "law and order" on the black poor) the limitation of the size and expenditures of the California state bureaucracy, whose dimensions are said to be a liberal plot against the free, enterprising, and creative individual. But this has been a conspicuous failure, especially when efforts have been made to seriously curtail expenditures for higher education, which is as prized a part of the life cycle of the organizational middle class as the doings of the students are a threat to its cultural identity.

The California experience indicates that the dossier society generates intense subjective anxieties and frustrations in the bulk of the population of that state, and that they can be exploited up to the point where immediate material interests are threatened. But these material interests, as structural features of the "New Industrial State," are what sustain the dossier society. The nondissenting classes will, for the immediate future, live with their feelings of helplessness and insignificance in the face of bureaucratic expertise, as well as with the discontinuity between their subjective realities and the realities of the organizational worlds which they inhabit. (It should be noted that George Wallace and his "American Independence Party" offer a more proletarian and frankly racist version of the same appeal, with the propaganda

endlessly mentioning "beauticians," "taxi drivers," and "little
people" in general.)

The organizational middle class and the unionized skilled proletariat are, as of now, nondissenting classes because their members
by and large believe that through one's individual efforts and hard
work one can (and should) increase his "share in America's prosperity"; and much of their energy, both physical and emotional, is
centered around the struggle to obtain or increase this share. Also,
for whatever reasons, they tend to believe in unquestioning acceptance of recognized ideologies and authorities. Consequently, they
have neither the energy nor the inclination to view the corporate
power structure as the cause of their oppression, nor to direct
action against it.

In the disaffected classes—the black and (increasingly) Latin
lower classes, as well as a growing proportion of middle-class youth
and their elders in the academic middle class—ever more predomi-
nant forms of consciousness depict the entire social order outside
their cultural enclaves as a seamless web of organized, interrelated,
manipulative, repressively dominating power which seems incapable of making any contact with their subjective realities or of
attributing any significance to those subjective realities.

The disaffected groups must pursue their social-political objectives and at the same time demonstrate dramatically that they
themselves are "real"—both to themselves and to what appears to
be an all-encompassing, all-devouring organizational monster.

The National Conference on New Politics, held in Chicago
August 31–September 3, 1967, adopted the resolution of the Black
Caucus. It indicates the development of consciousness: the need
to deny, repudiate, and reverse feelings of individual and group
powerlessness, or, rather, nonexistence.

> We strongly suggest that white civilizing committees be established
> immediately in all white communities to civilize and humanize the
> savage and beast-like character that runs rampant throughout
> America as exemplified by George Lincoln Rockwell and Lyndon
> Baines Johnson.

The whites must be made to experience the manifestations of
black subjective feeling with such intensity that they concede, with
sincere and emotional contrition, their collective responsibility for
the victimization of blacks.

The political epithets of the social movements of the 1960s tell their own story: "the system"; "the organized system" (introduced by Paul Goodman in *Growing up Absurd*); "power structure"; "white power structure" (abbreviated in Watts as "the WHIPS"); "establishment"; "white liberal establishment"; "corporate liberal establishment"; "establishment press"; "the machine" (used in reference to everything *in toto* that partakes of large-scale organization); "the apparatus." Some of these epithet-metaphors convey the impression that a ruling conspiratorial elite directs and profits from what is seen as the total domination of society (or a smaller unit, as in "downtown power structure" or "local establishment"—for that matter, even "the sociological establishment"). Others imply that what is perceived as the organizational juggernaut is under no one's control but its own. Always present are the elements of "power," in the sense of omnipotence, and "structure," in the sense of an ill-understood interlocking array of interlocking organizations through which power is exerted. One is left to imagine that all this confronts what must be a powerless and unstructured "people."

Potential rebels, dissenters, and malcontents can no longer, as I have already said, hope to compete with the sheer size and precision machinery of contemporary corporate and state structures. But in addition, the character of the social-political reality which each individual experiences subjectively is being drastically affected by the changing relationship of individuals to the streams of information emanating from, and gathered by, these giant organizations. On the one hand, it is becoming close to impossible for the mass of individuals to arrive at coherent, let alone accurate, notions of what large corporate and state organizations are actually *doing* at any given moment—or of what they have planned for the future. Most obviously, the sophistication of technology and the complexity of the economy and social order require that much of the public information on the activities and decisions of corporations and the state is necessarily of a highly technical nature and will certainly become even more technical in the future. A great deal of this information is incomprehensible to the layman without the assistance of experts in the natural and social sciences. Furthermore, this information is usually in such monumental profusion that the layman simply lacks the time to collect and organize it into an intelligent structure that he can grasp and manipulate; he must rely upon full-time specialists for that. For example, if he buys some shares of stock in a corporation manufacturing advanced electronic weaponry, he will not have the slighest notion of the workings of the products or the uses to which they might be put. He merely follows the advice of a stockbroker, who is at least briefed by economists and technical consultants, however much his counsel is actually based on rumors, hunches, or numerology. Having made a "good investment," the layman will be totally ignorant of the local political and economic impact of the corporation's Brazilian subsidiary, and he will similarly know nothing of the potential effect of the corporation's intrigues in Washington for the adoption of a still more deadly weapons system upon delicate negotiations with the Soviet Union for the limitation of the arms spiral.

The quantity, complexity, and inaccessibility of the information on the *routine* activities of large organizations are factors which would clearly inhibit the impact upon the mass of the population of comprehensive and abstract theories of institutional development and political, social, and economic causality. Moreover, the time-binding functions of consciousness are inhibited (should there be any capacity or desire to exercise them): activities and policies cannot be easily related to their origins or to their likely consequences—except, of course, by "qualified experts" whose qualifications and expertise may be in part assumed by outsiders for no better reason than their official positions and the volume of information which they release.

The war in Vietnam may well be one of the classic examples of this failure of the time-binding function among the American people as a whole. Leaving aside the considerable unconscious, subliminal, and indirect impact of the war, it appears that it was over a period of several years assimilated into consciousness among the adult population of all classes largely in the form of a minor nuisance. More acute concern arose only at times of major catastrophes or pronounced changes of the rules—"escalations"—by one side or the other. The historical, social, and political roots of the conflict and of American intervention in it were obscured by mounds of statistics—body counts; villages considered "pacified," "secure," or "under government control"; numbers of bombing missions flown; tons of bombs dropped, or "structures" destroyed; troop strengths of the various combatants; votes cast in rigged elections; acts of terrorism allegedly committed in given months, and so forth. On top of this there were torrents of explanations of United States and Saigon government policies, plans, and strategies couched in dense bureaucratic jargon; policy statements; optimistic predictions; exhortations to national unity and patriotism; shallow reportage; and ringing declarations emerging from multinational conferences of heads of state.

As a partial consequence of this inundation of information, even opponents of the war were driven to reacting situationally; after an initial period of shock following each major "escalation," they gradually accommodated themselves to the new situation as a "given" or constant factor and reformulated their policies in terms of it. They did not dare to think in terms of possible future "escalations," even though such "escalations" could be seen as implied by the inner logic of the war policy once they had actually taken place. As "escalations" occurred in an almost routine way, many opponents of the war, being kept constantly off balance and suspecting that traditional forms of political organization and pressure were ineffectual, gave way to feelings of apathy. Mad statistical gyrations in periodic polls and attitude surveys possibly indicated that numerous persons who did not actually oppose the war were afflicted by anxiety and confusion and were driven into sullen apathy rather than protest.

While it is by no means unusual for civilian populations to be deluded as to the military policies of their governments, surely there has never been a war so exhaustively reported and documented over so long a period, and generating such a mass of published detailed information representing so many different political viewpoints while the war itself was still in progress. The "information gap" between layman and expert conceivably, therefore, operated for long periods as a sort of indirect instrument of control, most strongly, of course, over those elements of the population for whom "Cold War" imagery retained its potency; and always provided that the routine progress of the war was not disrupted by major political or military catastrophes and other dramatic alterations of the status quo.

To recapitulate: organizational complexity, geographical dispersal, sophisticated technology, precision operations, elaborate planning, and extreme specialization of skilled personnel, as characteristic of the "mature" industrial corporations and the state (which together dominate the society), appear to render it difficult for outsiders, nonspecialists, persons below the "technostructure" level, and, quite possibly, large numbers of the more insular specialists within the organizations themselves, to understand the routine functioning of these organizations. To subscribe to a comprehensive theoretical model of social reality that at least *purports* to take into account the social and technological change of the past several decades (i.e., to identify explicity and doctrinally as a "post-Marxist," "Galbraithist," or perhaps "Technofascist"), such that all activities and divisions within the society could be at least described in its terms, and a guide to political action thereby obtained, would seem to be increasingly out of the question for most people, including intellectuals.

With the increasing obsolescence of the functional rationality underlying the mass politics of dissent and revolt which was characteristic of the Era of Industrialization in Europe and (to a lesser extent) the United States, the sort of comprehensive social-political ideologies propagated by the mass-organization type of social movement have lost a great deal of their former function. This is, of course, in addition to what was lost because of the affluence emerging in mass-consumption societies, and the consequent class peace between proletariat and capitalists. At the same time, some of these ideologists are becoming dated because of the intellectual rigidities of theoreticians as well as the ongoing processes of social change.

The result is not quite "The End of Ideology"; new ideologies exalting subjectivity and experience have appeared and seem to thrive among dissenting and rebellious youth everywhere in the industrialized world. To understand the causes of this trend, it is first necessary to return to the problem of information and consciousness.

Since the complexity of the new social reality reinforces the tendency to react situationally to organizational activities and policies, we often become aware of the existence of (or begin to evaluate seriously) major organized structures in our environment only when they undergo crisis or breakdown. Such mass awareness as may exist of the institutions comprising the international monetary system is undoubtedly attributable to the series of international monetary crises which began in 1964. Similarly, large numbers of people became conscious of the existence of the Northeast Power Grid only after the Great Power Failure of November 1965, when for several hours seventy million people in the United States and Canada were deprived of electric service. The military defeats in Vietnam that began on January 31, 1968, coinciding as they did with the opening of the presidential primary campaigning season in the United States and coming hard on the heels of a spectacular official propaganda campaign designed to sow optimism on the home front, compelled a renewed interest in the war among the mass of the American population—but with a new twist sufficient to terminate President Johnson's political career.

A significant component of subjective reactions to disasters incurred by remote, awesome, technologically sophisticated, and precisely coordinated organizations is that of *absurdity*, which I will define for my purposes as the simultaneous enforced juxtaposition in consciousness of two or more ideas, thoughts, or sensations that are mutually exclusive and flatly contradictory, both of which must be accepted as at least in part simultaneously true or real; and with the consequence that the coherence of the individual's subjective reality is undermined. What cannot be is; what cannot happen does. To a middle-class American enjoying record prosperity but unschooled in the arcana of international high finance, the idea that the dollar is somehow "in danger" is, on the face of it, absurd. The sight of New York City lying totally dark at midnight is absurd. Above all, a televised film clip of an air strike on Saigon represents just about the limit of absurdity. But there are other sources of the absurd, as we shall see.

I have said repeatedly that an individual may have to go far out of his way to gather even very partial information on what large corporations or the state are up to at any given moment. But there is, of course, other information with which these institutions bombard him deliberately and incessantly. We have already examined the problem of repressive consumption: in the mass-consumption economy, corporations must have guaranteed markets for products whose production is planned years in advance. New needs must be constantly created to make room for still more new products. The techniques of mass persuasion and publicity thus required have led to the creation of entire new industries and applied sciences. The consumer is made to feel the immediacy of the product; it is Now and it is New. He must gratify his appetite at once and forthwith in order to "be where the action is." Installment plans ("years to pay; only pennies a day"—"X now and pay later"), credit cards, long-term mortgages, and the like make the transfer of goods easy, swift, and painless in appearance. Such devices are indeed vital to the economy. Advertising even seeks to do away with the guilt which may be evoked by self-indulgence ("Come on, relax . . . you *owe* it to yourself to enjoy a . . .").

The cumulative effect of advertising and other forms of mass persuasion is a total assault upon bourgeois values. It discourages thrift—in fact, when typical lower middle-class consumers begin to save money in large quantities, this is regarded by economists as a danger signal, possibly foreshadowing a business slowdown in part because consumers fear one—sobriety, prudence, economy (Whatever happened to that word "cheap"?), industriousness, and respectability ("Test-drive the Wild Ones at your X dealer today!"). There can be no doubt that advertising cumulatively urges the consumer to place greater reliance upon subjective experience—even cigarettes and beer are indicated to have sexual allure—and to live absolutely in and for the present. The time-binding features of bourgeois culture such as "saving for a rainy day" and other deferred gratification patterns, devotion to duty, planning ahead, and the like, are obviously subject to erosion in favor of situational response patterns, immersion in a mindless present, and hedonism directed in such a manner as to maximize long-term economic growth.

The mass culture, then, offers pleasure but is clearly manipulated and regimented from without. In the mass culture it is important that you enjoy yourself, certainly, but it is equally important that you do not get left out! To join properly in all the fun, you have to own your own thingumabob with whatsit attachment or, better still, be the first kid/family (choose one) on your block with *two* of them.

The mass culture appeared to be making heavy inroads in the American middle class after World War II, though it never entirely replaced the older bourgeois values, especially in rural areas. The deepest penetration, according to popular stereotype and consensus among the social critics of the day, was made in the Levittown-type suburban subdivisions that were springing up around every major city. There one could find vast numbers of the rapidly growing organizational middle class, who were busily accumulatnig consumer goods, consumer debt, and children. The social critics of the early 1950s—a rather innocuous lot by present standards, since they were concentrating primarily upon the cultural misuse of affluence by the newly affluent—disgustedly regarded the suburbanites as a collection of vacuous, shallow, spineless, conformist careerists. In a country which was in the grip of an amorphous reactionary terror, and which still nostalgically honored the bourgeois virtues of "rugged individualism" and "self-reliance," it was perhaps to be expected that suburban conformity would be unconsciously settled upon as an acceptably noncontroversial controversial issue.

In that setting, the cultural impact of repressive consumption was obvious. Instances could always be found of persons who were terrified of ostracism for not having purchased some product, for having retained a model considered obsolete by their neighbors, or for having purchased a model considered excessively expensive, inexpensive, or otherwise departing conspicuously from local standards. Goods were purchased for children for fear that they would otherwise be judged "maladjusted" by other parents or school authorities. Isolated individuals with intellectual tastes in music or literature indulged themselves furtively. The arts of consumership and conformity ("life adjustment") were explicitly taught in schools.

The social critics of the 1950s, such as C. Wright Mills (*White Collar*), David Riesman (*The Lonely Crowd*), and William H. Whyte, Jr. (*The Organization Man*), remarked on the somewhat compulsive pose of contentment as well as on the naïve optimism and political apathy that they found in the new suburbs. Mills referred to "cheerful robots." By the end of the decade, intellectuals were virtually unanimous in stigmatizing the college-student children of the middle classes as "The Silent Generation."

CHAPTER 3

Phases of Cultural-Political Dissidence Among White Middle-Class Youth Since the Late 1950s

The Beat Generation (1956- or 1957–1960) was a subculture which began to form, broadly speaking, after the Korean War around small groups of poets, writers, artists, and musicians in Greenwich Village (New York City) and North Beach (San Francisco), with lesser concentrations in other large cities. In these places the Beats grew on the fringes of the "hipster" subculture of marijuana-smoking jazz musicians. The spread of the subculture depended heavily upon the media: Herb Caen, a *San Francisco Chronicle* columnist, invented the word "beatnik" in 1957. Welcome or not, the word "beatnik" provided an identity for several thousand students and dropouts, some of whom could be found hanging around on the cultural and geographic fringe of every large university or small liberal-arts college outside of the South; every campus was said to have its "beatnik hangout." In contrast to the ideology of joy preached by the freaks of the middle 1960s, the beatniks of the 1950s affected an appearance of suffering and torment, and complained that they were being driven insane or crushed by conventional society, with its bureaucratized existence, sterile materialism, and "conformity." Some of the visible consequences of this constituted a sort of sterile mirror image of the mass culture: if the latter valued cleanliness, neatness, and "good posture," the beatniks had to be filthy, sloppy, and slouchy. This subculture generated, nevertheless, a sort of mass appeal based on its mystique of sexual freedom and on the fact that, while it was fashionable among students and intellectuals to denounce "conformity," the beatniks were the only ones *visibly* not conforming. (Or, to turn it around, those who were visibly not "conforming" were classified as beatniks.)

Overt political activism in the colleges was at this time mostly limited to feeble stirrings on the issue of nuclear disarmament. Much more impressive were local outbursts over the question of sexual freedom (euphemized by the use of such phrases as "the social code," "parietal hours," and *in loco parentis*). Such outbursts were not at the time defined as "political."

In the period before 1960, the beatniks, as Jack Newfield writes in *A Prophetic Minority,* a book on the New Left, "were the only rebellion in town." But the willingness of masses of youths to consider the beards, folk music, bad poetry, and worse novels of the beatniks as exciting forms of rebellion was the first indication that a social movement of a new type was emerging. The existence of the Reality Gap and the distinctive cultural features of this movement (as well as of the black movement)—spontaneity, fear of organization, subjectivism, totalistic antiauthoritarianism, the liberation of repressed existence—were foreshadowed by the Beats on the one hand and the "alienated youth" studied by Kenneth Keniston on the other.

Keniston studied twelve individuals—not known to each other —of this latter type at Harvard University in the late 1950s. His book *The Uncommitted,* based on this study, describes what would later become recognizable as essential features of freak-consciousness as "major themes of alienation." For example, his subjects were exclusively concerned with the present, with subjective states, emotions, perceptions; they sought to break through artificial barriers and conventional categories in order to have direct contact with reality; and they had an overwhelming need for self-expression, not to reveal themselves to others, but to justify or affirm themselves.[1] In their pessimism about the future, these "alienated youths" are comparable to the freak-radicals of the 1960s who fear fascist repression when they do not expect the immediate Apocalypse. Also, as turbulent freak-radical mass actions indicate, "adventure" can be the other side of the coin of "sentience" in the same individual. Keniston also describes a "fragmentation of identity" in his subjects, an inability to commit themselves to any external object or person, an inability to make choices, and the subjective experience of themselves as nonexistent.[2] These "alienated youths," having a primitive impulse toward "fluidity," were like isolated individuals, without any prospect of imagining any social force which would champion that impulse. The freak, as we shall show, sees himself as that social force ("We are the people!") and derives his identity from being "into" his "thing." He is committed to nothing but the condition and principle of "fluidity" itself, and regards all social arrangements which are founded on the primacy of organizational necessities (i.e., the system) as "social slavery" and as presenting him with a "freedom" which is a mere sham and delusion.

The inauguration of the "direct action" phase of the "civil rights" movement, with the invention of the sit-in in Greensboro, North Carolina, in February 1960, touched off a sudden outburst of emotion on the campuses. The issue of nuclear disarmament had been socially disembodied: while immediate financial benefits of the war industries had trickled down in Keynesian fashion to practically everyone in the society, nobody not motivated by the most abstract sort of idealism could have any use for "peace." The black movement provided the possibility of "action" of potentially national significance, action that was dramatic, demanded physical courage, and was, above all, morally unambiguous; it was defined as worthy of total involvement ("commitment") to the degree that it contrasted with bureaucratized society. The emotional reaction to the drama of the black movement also energized the issue of nuclear disarmament (until the Test Ban Treaty of 1963, after which it subsided) and spread to stirrings on the issue of what was vaguely called "university reform."

The ensuing cultural phase, the Old New Left (1960–1965), was almost at its inception conceptualized as a "student movement," and right from the beginning it seemed to be defining itself through sheer action, a certain visible nonconformity in life-style (the press rapidly invented the stereotype of the bearded "peacenik"), and abhorrence of confinement in either formal structures or formal doctrines. Intellectuals and critics of the Left decried action without a broader conception of strategy and tactics, advocated greater organizational discipline and continuity on issues, and demanded more coordination, better leadership, and a more sharply defined "ideology." It was assumed by the more optimistic that all these things would come with greater maturity; this, of course, has not happened and shows few signs of doing so. Others, like Phillip Altbach, national chairman of the Student Peace Union, felt able to deny that a movement existed at all:

> The recent rash of student activity on the campuses of the United States has created the illusion of a student movement of substantial proportions, but a serious and critical look at the situation will be adequate proof that, although a student movement is needed and wanted, it does not actually exist. There is no force on the student scene that can sustain action or concern on a particular issue. Despite the efforts of some of the leaders of the liberal community, the American student movement is a myth.[3]

That the movement was a myth in 1961 was perfectly true; it can still be true now, but there is nothing wrong with this. In contemporary social movements, myths transmitted and sustained within subcultures are more important than organizational structures.

On the other hand, the early activities heaped scorn and contempt upon the beatniks in language almost identical with that used by a later generation of New Leftists against the hippies; Beats were regarded as an extreme form of what was considered to be a national disease of political passivity and "apathy."

The accession of the Kennedy Administration to office (or perhaps, one should say, to the Throne) fostered the *image* and *myth* of some sort of amorphous forward development allied with youthful energy. Activists in the "Movement" accordingly spoke of some vague generalized "change" (a concept every bit as mystical as "revolution" was to become in a later period) but it was not considered out of the question that the "power structure" might be pressured into making it. According to the "Port Huron Statement," SDS's 1962 founding manifesto, it was important to remain on speaking terms with liberals because of their "relevance." (In 1962 the word "relevant," when used by a New Leftist, described somebody who knew somebody who knew a power-holder; now, the same word, when used by a liberal, describes somebody who

knows somebody who knows a New Leftist or a "black militant.")
It was thought to be ludicrous to suggest that students or youth represented an independent social interest; it appeared more sensible
that students should assist the black movement where possible, and
revive the energies of the industrial working class and the liberals.
Thus Tom Hayden, et al., in the "Port Huron Statement" called for
a campus-based "new left" to create a "new politics"—a condition
in which a universally aroused citizenry, having shaken off
"apathy," would "participate" actively in all structures in which
they found themselves, and so prod these structures into new social
policies with the further objective of creating changes in "human
relationships." The "new left" was to be a little wheel which, in
spinning rapidly, would nudge a more cumbersome larger wheel
into motion; it was to "start controversy across the land."

By 1963–1964 a new subphase had been entered in which the
moralistic posturings and intellectualizing of the activists of 1960–
1962 had become de-emphasized and the ideal of "movement"
work had become "going South" for the then biracial Student
Nonviolent Coordinating Committee, or "organizing the poor" in
an urban slum in something like SDS's Education Research and
Action Projects (ERAP). Since SDS used a class analysis of poverty, it tried to organize poor whites in such entities as JOIN—
Jobs or Income Now, in Chicago—as well as blacks in Boston,
Cleveland, and Newark. The entity in the latter city was NCUP
(the Newark Community Union Project), the most successful of
the ERAP projects, but in fact not very successful. The work in
the South was by far the most dangerous and glamorous. The activists lived "fluidly"; the white activists assimilated black culture in
varying degrees and exuded a mystique of personal and sexual
freedom. Campus activism was likely to be centered around local
CORE chapters and campus-based integrationist groups; these
entities often contained more white students and intellectuals than
blacks, and they frequently imitated slavishly and pointlessly the
tactics which had grown out of immediate experiences in the South.

Totalistic impulses in the white movement were reflected in
such concepts as "participatory democracy," "dialogue," and "creative disorder"—all subsequently adopted by the state, the first as
"maximum feasible participation" by the Office of Economic Opportunity and the latter by the Peace Corps; a similar fate subse-

quently befell "student power," which has been adopted by more moderate students in order to outmaneuver SDS. As a political theory this never amounted to much, since the principal function of this rhetoric was not theory. Student power was a verbalization to try to nullify or eliminate structure hierarchical controls from particular environments in which people happened to find themselves. Where "participatory democracy" was represented as a political theory it was then, in accordance with the fashionable consensus established by the political scientists, regarded as having something to do with the "decision-making process." The original formulation in the "Port Huron Statement" begins with a paragraph in which the subjective impulse is manifest, although its potential applicability to the modification of institutions is disembodied and mystical:

> We would replace power rooted in possession, privilege, or circumstance by power and uniqueness rooted in reflectiveness, reason, and creativity. As a *social system* we seek the establishment of a democracy of individual participation governed by two central aims: that the individual share in those social decisions determining the quality and direction of his life; that society be be organized to encourage independence among men and provide the media for their common participation.[4]

This quickly became reduced to a formula or ritual incantation such as "People should have control over the decisions which affect their lives," with several possible variations thereupon. But by 1965, "participatory democracy" was intended as a descriptive term for a type of scene, way of life, and subculture developed in local organizing projects, both in the North and in the South:

> . . . it becomes necessary to think of a project from the beginning, not merely as a tool for social change, but as a community. The community is made up both of people from the neighborhood and of staff persons who, on a long-term basis, so far as they can become part of the neighborhood. The spirit of a community, as opposed to an organization, is not, We are together to accomplish this or that end, but, We are together to face whatever life brings.[5]

The end of the Old New Left as a cultural phase may perhaps have been foreshadowed by Bob Dylan's abandonment in 1964 of the writing of protest songs, followed by his championing of introspection and celebration of the drug culture. In any case, the end

came swiftly after the dying down of the Free Speech Movement
outburst at the University of California at Berkeley (1964–1965).
In part, this crisis itself reflected the exhaustion of the political
imagination and forward thrust of the "civil rights" movement in
both South and North; the energies and attention of activists and
their sympathizers were "brought back home" to focus on repressed existence within the university itself. The students had
drawn analogies between the black population and themselves; the
tactics and rationale of the mass sit-ins were used in their own
behalf. Politics was not the class struggle but, as in the "civil
rights" movement, the disruption of the institutional machine by
the powerless. As Mario Savio put it during the mass sit-in in
Sproul Hall (December 2, 1964; it was ended by a mass arrest
which precipitated the collapse of the "educational process"):

> There is a time when the operation of the machine becomes so
> odious, makes you so sick at heart that you can't take part; you
> can't even tacitly take part, and you've got to put your bodies upon
> the levers, upon all the apparatus, and you've got to make it stop.
> And you've got to indicate to the people who run it, to the peo-
> ple who own it, that unless you're free, the machine will be pre-
> vented from working at all.

While the present-day student radicals are often condemned
by academics for "brownshirt tactics," "Stalinist intimidation," or
"McCarthyism of the Left," the fact is that the specific idea-content
is not of significance. When they complain that the course work is
not "meaningful" or that they cannot "relate" to it, this is an assertion that the total context in which the idea is communicated is of
greater significance to the students than is the intellectual value.
To carry this to its logical conclusion, any two ideas expounded in
the same auditorium to the same audience by different authority-
figures standing in the same power relation to that audience would
be equally insignificant by comparison with the impulse of that
audience to dissolve the speaker-audience relationship. And the
important thing about a course in revolution is not the "revolution"
but its "course" context. When New York Newsreel (a New Left
film-making outfit) condemned the 1968 New York City Film
Festival as "bourgeois," they were not referring to the films being
shown so much as the fact that the festival was being held in the
plush surroundings of Lincoln Center; the film art was being con-

sumed as part of the life-style of the upper middle class; it was held to be necessary to abolish this life-style, film festivals, and the films intended to be shown at the festivals.

Indications of emerging freak-consciousness were also apparent in such manifestations as the "Filthy Speech Movement," consisting of weird-looking individuals who were convinced that the right of free political advocacy on university property—the stated objective of the FSM—included the right to carry a sign reading "FUCK." The FSM also marked the official emergence of the freak as a social problem—in the guise of the "nonstudent."

The consequences of political frustration and defeat upon the Old New Left began to form something of a pattern: SNCC, having seen the Mississippi Freedom Democratic Party refused full official recognition at the 1964 Democratic Convention at Atlantic City, lapsed into a collective traumatic shock marked by the emergence of a "freedom high" function which believed in the cultural awakening of the black farmers of the South through music, poetry, and art. SDS, having failed to make a discernible impact upon the sensitivity to the "escalation" of the war in Vietnam through campus "teach-ins" or a mass demonstration in Washington on April 17, 1965, experimented with such slogans as "Make love not war." Two former "civil rights" activists in the South founded the Sexual Freedom League in Berkeley. Joe Macdonald, a Berkeley protest singer, became the leader of Country Joe and the Fish, the rock group; meanwhile, the Free Speech Movement, by late spring, 1965, was sinking into the ground.

On a broader scale, the drug culture, acid-rock music, and other elements of a new culture phase were consolidating into hippieism (1965–1967).

The word "hippie" had been in use in the early 1960s in hipster-beatnik parlance to describe a young naive would-be hipster; it had the same meaning associated with the word "teeny-bopper" several years later. The Beat subculture had continued to exist, perhaps had grown; there the development of hippieism had been an organic growth. Among masses of other people, the historical circumstances in which hippieism presented a cultural alternative may have been unusually propitious: overt politics was a failure, while organized society every day appeared more insane and out of control. The shift in cultural outlook is probably under-

standable in the light of other historical experiences involving the
frustration of overt politics. Bertram D. Wolfe has described the
cultural aftermath of the abortive Revolution of 1905 among
Russian students:

> Among the young, eroticism and suicide became mass phe-
> nomena, embraced with the same headlong extremism that had
> been given to revolution. The brief celebrity of Artsybashev's
> *Sanin* (published in 1907) was due to the fact that it combined
> both themes in one. Two suicides, two seductions, a glowing de-
> scription of nudity, a toying with incest; the glorification of bodily
> strength, voluptuousness, physical joys; the ridiculing of those
> who waste their time on politics or knowledge; the admonition to
> live like animals, follow instinct and impulse, abandon principles,
> plans, regrets, and to use reason only as devil's advocate and
> instrument for liberating oneself from all codes, conventions and
> principles—such is Saninism. It was as symbolic of its moment as
> the nihilism of *Fathers and Sons* had been for the sixties of the
> preceding century.[6]

The spread of the drug culture did not overtly reduce political
activity. SDS grew rapidly in size throughout the 1965–1967 period. But by the summer of 1965, "going South" was said to be
"not happening," and within another year the growing strength of
Black Nationalist ideologies and the increasing number of ghetto
rebellions threatened to cut off white activists from all contact with
radical blacks (who told them to "organize your own communities"); this left considerable confusion and bitterness. Some student
energies were absorbed in assisting Mexican-American grape strik-
ers in California; older "community organizers" found jobs in
Office of Economic Opportunity "community action" projects or
returned to colleges and graduate schools. Opposition to the war in
Vietnam and to conscription continued to develop throughout the
1965–1967 period, though without the slightest indication of any
impact on the policies of the State. By 1967, the spread of the drug
culture on the campuses had led to talk of so-called "Movement
dropouts," and both student activists and hippies shared the
"Flower Power" slogan. Meanwhile, the number of hippies and
hippified students and teen-agers had grown to the point of making
possible those mass manifestations called "be-ins."

The World's First Human Be-In was held in San Francisco's
Golden Gate Park in late January 1967 and attracted twelve to

thirteen thousand people. An even larger one was held in the Sheep Meadow in Central Park in New York City on Easter Sunday, 1967. The *East Village Other*'s reporter heard somebody banging on a garbage can and was reminded of Marshall McLuhan's notion of the Tribal Drum, i.e., that in the Electronic Age there is a return to a primitive, amorphous, and communal form of solidarity and collective action:

> Sun and people, it was the best thing around. Anytime was a good time all day. But the best time was somewhere between 8:00 and noon. Early on, the meadow was all hippie, and the good vibrations all over, you swam in them. Somebody upended an empty orange sanitation drum, and that poor goddamn drum never stopped throbbing all day. Another raga—everybody synched in with it, everybody goddammit, and stayed synched all day. The drum was the focus of the good virbrations—you could actually tell who was synched in by the way the hippies grooved with the rhythm in every time we moved, everything we said, the way we wore our faces . . . five-dimensional raga. . . .
>
> Do your thing at the Be-In, that's all, everybody else does. Gregariousness isn't quite the word for it. Because nobody infiltrated anyone else's thing, except as part of his own thing. Like, people grinned like happy idiots at each other all day, exchanged flowers and stones and curtain rings and kisses, grooving together in LSD raga, but everybody was doing his very own personal thing. Friends did their thing together, Be-In acquaintances likewise, but the Tribal Drum was the only thing that held all twenty-thirty thousand of us really together. . . .[7]

A be-in was an unrestricted total event spontaneously created by the participants while each engaged in self-creation and expression. It had a significance for hippies strongly paralleling the expression of blacks in ghetto rebellions, but obviously differing in the intensity with which the subcultural identity was expressed in struggle against the cultural-political enemy.

The black dissident experiences repressed existence as material deprivation and as the agony of living in a white cultural-political universe; his white counterpart experiences it as boredom and triviality. But immemorial custom among left-wing radicals requires a reference to "justice" or, better, "social justice." For a white child of affluence to associate such rhetoric with boredom or other grievances reflecting his actually experienced "reality of everyday life" would be ludicrous on the face of it, and in any

case would have nothing to do with his unprecedented desires for
the realization of unprecedented possibilities (blacks, chicanos, and
Puerto Ricans can, however, speak of "justice" so long as they
remain submerged castes). Inevitably, therefore, the joy marking
mass campus freak-outs is accompanied by expressions of righteous
indignation over "imperialism" and "racism." It is not until a university administration can be subjectively associated with one of
the recognized "injustices," either by virtue of the school's insti-
tional linkages or for having punished some of their white students
for having acted in the name of a moral absolute (breaking a few
university rules in the process), that any considerable number of
students will permit themselves to break loose from the academic
routine. The conventional culture denies them the conceptual tools
with which to legitimize in their own minds their impulses to rebel
in their own self-interest; there are no standards for judging the
rationality (as opposed to the *acceptability*) of boredom, triviality,
or garden-variety authoritarianism; it is difficult to attack "efficiency" as a value when applied to a particular case. On the one
hand they are condemned as "spoiled" and subjected to "when-I-
was-your-age" lectures; on the other hand a Stokely Carmichael
tells them: "You're fighting for the right to smoke pot while we're
fighting for our lives." So, at San Francisco State College:

> The energy with which the BSU [Black Students Union] pur-
> sued the attack on institutional racism had both an invigorating
> and an overwhelming impact on the white movement. On the one
> hand, the discovery of racism in the institution gave the white
> movement an entire new area to pour energy into, and attracted
> new groups of people. On the other hand, the whites' insecurity
> as to the exact specifications of racism meant in practice that
> blacks had to be called in to do the defining at every critical point.
> First gradually, then rapidly as the strike action began, the white
> movement became the satellite of the nonwhite.
>
> At the outset of the strike, the SDS and SDS/PL leadership
> won adoption of the position that white students would put for-
> ward no demands. This political line put the white non-leadership
> in the peculiar position not only of having no analysis to articulate,
> but of being committed to allowing none to be articulated.
>   (Martin Nicolaus, "S.F. State: History Takes a Leap,"
>   *Movement, February 1969.*)

Overt formulations within SDS of conceptions of white students' autonomous revolutionary self-interest are not lacking. The following reflects the viewpoint of the New Working Class faction:

> Youth, and particularly students, can . . . reject the system as a whole. As trainees in a system of exploitation, their rejection of the role of trainee is a rejection not simply of the specific task they are being trained for, but a rejection of the process as a whole. This includes a rejection of consumer culture and manipulative consumption as well as the rejection of meaningless work they refuse to participate in (viz., the hippies). It can extend— has begun to extend—to a global critique of American capitalism's role both at home and abroad.
>
> Youth, as the object of intense socialization of education, are best able to perceive the potential that socialized production contains. Yet they are being trained for individual roles as workers and consumers that are boring, uncreative, wasteful. The perception of this fundamental gap between potential and reality leads youth to radical consciousness. And we have already begun to develop alternatives to the existing system. In the liberated buildings of Columbia, in the dropout communities of New York, San Francisco, and dozens of other cities, we are beginning to build our own commonwealth, our own culture.
>
> (Dave Gilbert, "Consumption: Domestic Imperialism— A New Left Introduction to the Political Economy of American Capitalism," SDS pamphlet, 1968.)

If the radical rejects the "system as a whole," his task is not to improve the "educational process" but to prevent it. Research, scholarship, specialized training, and the transmission and storage of "knowledge" are construed as in the service of alien powers which depend upon the university for the continuing fabrication of human, intellectual, and technical-discovery products.

Among those who participate in the "Movement's" rejection of the educational process there are very few "intellectuals" (as this term is commonly used; I will forgo definitions). The men who most closely approach intellectuals among the articulate spokesmen of the movement are less describable as men of ideas than as men adroit in combining rhetoric and adrenalin. Intellectual idols— Paul Goodman, Frantz Fanon, Che Guevara, Timothy Leary, Herbert Marcuse—are adopted as fads of the season, as much for their saintly or heroic personal qualities as for their ideas, and then forgotten. Dissent is not what you say or think; it is something you do with your body. In November 1963, Chuck McDew of SNCC said, "You say you give us your support. We ask you: Where is your body?" A little over four years later Jerry Rubin said, "Politics is how you live your life, not whom you support or whom you vote for." An individual's politics—or, rather, the political significance of his actions—is to be assessed in the context of an evaluation of all the energies which he expends. Expounding the viewpoint of the New Left or explaining the significance of the "underground" press is therefore not radical, since most of the person's energies are locked up in following the rules of the interview format, and the program can be safely consumed on a rather superficial level by the viewing audience. By the same logic, saying "fuck" or picking one's nose on television is radical, since one is more completely involved in destroying the sanitized and disinfected format of the show.

It is possible that only a movement of the American white middle class could come up with a slogan like "Make Love Not War." The white middle class, of course, is characteristically trained in impulse control, which does not so much enforce abstinence as it enforces compartmentalization, i.e., a generalized commandment to the effect that THOU SHALT NOT FUCK ON COMPANY TIME. (Hence the cultural significance of the "office Christmas party," when there *is* fucking on company time and the office hierarchy is dissolved in alcohol.) Thus, as complex consciousness is developed in middle-class youth, a vague suspicion is generated to the effect that overt sexuality and the institution of the family have been turned into the manipulated extensions of "the system"—and of the consumer-goods industries in particular.

In traditional bourgeois culture, overt sexuality was construed as a sort of commodity relation, with women constituting the Supply and men constituting the Demand. That some such thing is in fact a function of institutions like *Playboy* magazine (circulation: over four million copies every month) and its imitators is quite well known; a glance through the pages of this magazine will always reveal pictures of naked, balloon-breasted young women juxtaposed to pictures of naked cameras, naked stereo sets, naked sports cars, and other voluptuous consumer goods. Against this background it became rational for freak dissidence, beginning with the "Love Generation," to include as an integral feature the intrusion of defiantly unmanipulated overt sexuality and nudity into every conceivable context that, by conventional norms, appears to be erotically disinfected.

In hippie politics the objective (or, more precisely, the inner logic) was not to "put your bodies on the levers" of the machine and so stop its functioning; rather it was to (as the title of an essay in the Chicago *Seed* put it) "Freak Out the Machine," to incite the enemy to self-injury through cultural destruction and the scrambling of meanings. For this it helped to maximize one's degree of individual disorientation from the conventional culture and the most extreme kinds of weirdness in communication, while paying as little attention as possible to the cultural-political enemy, attacking him primarily by means of the irrelevance of one's behavior toward the threat he represented. Therefore the hippies strove for total communication, painted each other, would be urged to come to "A Seething Conscious-Expanding Total Environmental Psychedelic Light-Show Dance," bought "psychedelic" rock records featuring electronic music and other exotic sounds and surrounded by "total album" packaging, or wore blue- or oranged-tinted glasses. Verbal and print communication was mistrusted as most tied to the conventional reality (and to the "straight" culture's "linear" and "compartmentalized" thought patterns); it was contaminated by past and present manipulation by the enemy. The hippies came up with such slogans as "May the Baby Jesus Open Your Mind and Shut Your Mouth," and "LEAVE ALL WORDS AND PHRASES BEHIND AND SAY SOMETHING." The nonviolent "Flower Power" posture must similarly be interpreted as a means of aggression used to confuse and ridicule the "straights" and their violent culture. American conventional culture lays enormous stress on personal violence. (Our murder rate, for example, is exceeded in the entire world by only three or four small Latin American republics.) The freaks, as before them the blacks, quickly abandoned nonviolence as soon as its utility as a means of aggression was exhausted.

According to Burton H. Wolfe,[8] a San Francisco Digger named Peter Berg, while fantasizing on an acid trip on March 21, 1967, accidentally started a rumor to the effect that a hundred thousand hippies were to descend on the city during the summer. The rumor process doubled the figure to two hundred thousand within the few hours preceding the story's publication in the *San Francisco Chronicle*. Local panic ensued. In any case, it is indisputable that a myth of nationwide proportions was created about an Apocalyptic "Summer of Love" in San Francisco. There was an influx, though nowhere near two hundred thousand and no more than a few thousand at any one time. "Genuine" hippies had been said, for months previously, to have been trying to escape the presence of cultural pollution wrought by "plastic hippies" and "teenyboppers." The self-protective capacities of the local scene were already overloaded; the newcomers were left to subsist in squalor or else go home immediately; morals collapsed. Persecution on the streets (micropolitics) combined with ghetto rebellions and the war in Vietnam (macropolitics) to create a sense of impending doom and cultural obsolescence.

Hippieism was the only culture phase ever to hold a formal funeral for itself; this was a "Death of Hippie" march, complete with coffin, through the streets of San Francisco in late September 1967. Recall the rock musician Jim Morrison's casual equation of "where we were" with "what was happening." While The Doors were composing "Strange Days," in the fall of 1967, other rock groups, as if indeed listening to the Tribal Drum, were burying hippieism. "The Red Sox Are Winning," by Earth Opera, is a song of despair and futility. The last lines are "In the year of the war/ The Red Sox are winning." An orator exclaims, "Let's make Boston America's number one baseball city!" The crowd responds with fascistic shouts of "Kill the hippies! Kill the hippies!" The Mothers of Invention album *We're Only in This for the Money* contains several songs satirizing and ridiculing hippies for shallowness, commercialism, idiotic perversions of the drug culture, and the shortcomings of nonviolence ("I will love the police while they kick the shit out of me on the street"). The Bee Gees came up with a hit song called "Back to Massachusetts," about a youth who hitched a ride to San Francisco "to do that thing I had to do," but who is now going back to Massachusetts.

The present culture phase, the New New Left, otherwise known as "The Revolution," "The Guerrilla Generation," and so forth, was consolidated during Stop the Draft Week (October 16–21, 1967), which culminated in the Pentagon Confrontation (October 21–22) in Washington. Indeed, the consolidation of a new culture phase may turn out to be the main historical significance of these events.

The principal mass manifestation of this new phase is the "confrontation," a nonspecific event in which everyone does his "thing" (clergymen pray, poets chant, guerrillas stage commando raids or fight police, and Trotskyites sell *The Militant*). The event can either be announced in advance or occur spontaneously; in either case, it is spontaneously created by the participants on the spot in accordance with past experience and present necessities. The point is not to put one's body on the levers of the machine, or to freak out the machine, but to smash the machine "by any means necessary," with the operative word being "any." For the freak-rebel, a confrontation is a be-in with an enemy whom it is necessary to fight rather than ignore. Abbie Hoffman, who manages to keep "in phase" (he was, successively, a SNCC working in Mississippi, a New York Digger, and a cofounder of the Yippies), says:

> We feel that the pig Pigasus, the Yippie candiate for president, has captured the imagination of the American public, and we plan to see that he is elected and inaugurated on January 20th, and we're gonna use any means necessary to effect that goal.
>
> We say . . . any means necessary . . . of course the overground immediately says, VIOLENCE, YOU MEAN VIOLENCE! And we say, no man, we mean any means necessary means any means necessary. They've got this violence hang-up out there. . . . You say, there'll be an action, and they think violence. It's unbelievable. Maybe they watch too many Westerns and shoot-ups. . . .
>
> My concept of revolution: I don't believe in confrontation politics. I believe in a politics of being. You go out and do whatever you have to do, and like cops who come in and smash you—that's their thing—so you fuck it, you just have to get out and do it and forget about the critics, and forget about those that are going to applaud and gonna dig. Fuck 'em and do it.[9]

The advent of the new culture phase was followed by a reaction against the overblown baroque pretentiousness of "psychedelic" rock in favor of a reversion to the "hard," primitive, scruffy, defiantly erotic and thoroughly nonrespectable style of an earlier period, as befitted a shift from cortical to glandular rebellion. Thus came forth songs of political subversion such as the Rolling Stones' enormously popular "Street Fighting Man."

A more detailed analysis of this new phase appears in the last chapter.

. . . and this is where it is . . .

A RULING CLASS CAN BE OVERTHROWN BUT A SYSTEM IS VULNERABLE EVERYWHERE AND NOWHERE.

ATTACK THE RULE BECAUSE IT EXISTS, THE POLICY BECAUSE IT IS PLANNED, THE DECISION BECAUSE IT IS MADE, THE PROCESS BECAUSE IT GOES ON, THE POWER BECAUSE IT IS THERE, AND THE SYSTEM BECAUSE IT FEELS BAD. ENJOY YOURSELF.

APOCALYPSE NOW—ALL THE CRAZIES ON THE LOOSE—THE MEANS JUSTIFY THE MEANS.

BUT WHAT DO YOU HOPE TO ACCOMPLISH? YOU SOUND LIKE MY MOTHER. BUT WHAT IS YOUR PROGRAM? I AM NOT TV GUIDE.

TABLE I. A COMPARISON OF THREE RECENT SOCIAL
MOVEMENTS CONTRASTING BUREAUCRATIZED
AND SUBCULTURAL DISSIDENCE

	Western European Communism (1920–1940)	**Western European Fascism (1920–1940)**	**"The Movement"— USA, 1960–? (especially after 1967)**
TYPE OF IDEOLOGY	Rationalist—supposedly based on determination of objective social reality	Irrationalist—determination of objective social reality thought to impede "will," "vital forces," etc.	Subjectivist—reality determined by individuals on the basis of experience
LEGITIMATION OF IDEOLOGY	"Scientific" determination of objective interests of the "proletariat"	Bankruptcy and incompetence of existing doctrines and their adherents	Adherence to an "ideology" unacknowledged
ARTICULATION OF MOVEMENT	Regimented bureaucratic mass organization	Regimented bureaucratic mass organization	Subcultural "globules"; informal associations of individuals, sustained by intense interaction, where a new "life-style" is practiced and developed
FAVORITE RECRUITING GROUNDS	Industrial working class	Lower middle class and other categories whose status or economics are threatened by economic collusion and/or social revolution; individuals such as demobilized soldiers and gangsters, whose status was nonexistent to begin with	Youth of white middle class

	Western European Communism (1920–1940)	Western European Fascism (1920–1940)	"The Movement"— USA, 1960–? (especially after 1967)
RECRUITMENT DEVICES	Building organization by propagandizing already discontented groups in hopes of increasing membership	Building organization by propagandizing already discontented groups in hopes of increasing membership	Exposure to sex, drugs, and music by peers leading to dissatisfaction with social conditions and vice versa
BONDS OF SOLIDARITY	Membership in formal organization, "party discipline," identification with the working class, symbols and trappings of the organization, familiarity with party doctrines and "political line," reliance for protection and/or improvement of conditions on the political power and organizational resources of the party apparatus	Membership in formal organization, "party discipline," identification with the nation / Leader / race/ "folk-community" / etc., symbols and trappings of the organization, familiarity with party doctrines and "political line," reliance for protection and/or career on the political power and organizational resources of the party apparatus	Close friendship with peers and intense involvement in the subculture, distinctive physical appearance and gestures ("V" signs, upraised fists, addressing strangers as "brother" and "sister" on the basis of outward appearance rather than known political beliefs)
LEGITIMATION OF TACTICS	The end justifies the means	The end justifies the means	The means justify the means
LEGITIMATION OF THE VANGUARD	"We know what the people (or proletariat) would know if they only knew enough"	"We will what the people would will if they were strong enough"	"We feel what the people would feel if they could feel enough"

	Western European Communism (1920–1940)	Western European Fascism (1920–1940)	"The Movement"— USA, 1960–? (especially after 1967)
PLACE OF THE INDIVIDUAL	Tool to be shaped and used for the fulfillment of the grand design of History	Tool to be shaped and used for the fulfillment of the grand design of the Leader	Encouraged to do anything he wants so long as he enjoys it and it does not harm other members of the subculture
HEROES AND MARTYRS	Workers, peasants and party members who organize the party, lead strikes, die on the barricades or are callously killed by the authorities Are willing to do or sacrifice anything for the party and the working class	Soldiers and uniformed party members who exemplify raw power and untrammeled will Are willing to do or sacrifice anything for the Leader and the party	Gurus, prophets, seers, holy men, saints, rebels who enjoy the revolution and who detest all authority on principle, rebels who prove their readiness to die (especially by getting killed), people who live without restraint, people who radiate "inner beauty"
LEGITIMATION OF ELITE	Master political strategists and tacticians, experts in application of theoretical doctrines to "concrete situations"	Superhuman attributes (as racial specimens, soldiers, visionaries, etc., who recognize no limitations on the use of violence) as allegedly manifested in their success in getting away with whatever they do	None; great suspicion of "power freaks" and "ego trips"; leaders deny being leaders

	Western European Communism (1920–1940)	Western European Fascism (1920–1940)	"The Movement"— USA, 1960–? (especially after 1967)
TYPE OF CONSCIOUSNESS DEVELOPED	"True consciousness," including identification with the proletariat and the "vanguard of the proletariat," understanding of the inexorable "laws" of historical development, rejection of opposing doctrines and hostile cultural manifestations as "bourgeois ideology" and "false consciousness"	Blind worship of Leader, intense nationalism, "race consciousness," intense hatred of real and fantasy enemies of nation or "race"	"Turning on to where it's at"— understanding of a provisional political truth which emerges from efforts to safeguard the continuing development of the self

In the horror of our modern life, there is nothing more difficult to verify than the root of a fact.

—*Norman Mailer* ("Open Letter to Richard Nixon," *Newsweek,* December 9, 1968, p. 87)

PART II

THE SOCIAL ORIGINS
OF DUAL CONSCIOUSNESS

CHAPTER 4

Introducing the Reality Gap

A conventional reality is generally shared and accepted throughout a society as "knowledge" of what is politically "real" (i.e., what is conventionally accepted as the objective reality of the social order, without necessarily implying legitimacy, approval, or even validity —"the free enterprise system"), or politically relevant; also, as rules of thumb as to what "makes sense." Intense class- and interest-group conflicts are compatible with the maintenance of the conventional reality intact; governments could be violently challenged without precluding the possibility that people on each side could say, "It figures!"

The maintenance of the conventional reality presupposes the operation of agencies or devices of socialization which reconcile the subjective experiences derived from daily life—which are likely to vary greatly if only because of different kinds of daily lives within a complex social order, not to mention individual differences—to what is conventionally accepted as objective social reality. In highly complex societies, subjective experiences of different environments may be highly discontinuous both from each other and from the "objective reality," the existence of which is generally insisted upon. Nobody really *experiences* "the democratic process," "the free market economy," "creeping inflation" (though we do experience a slow rise in prices, which is somehow not quite the same thing), or "the balance of payments."

As what is represented to be "objective social reality" becomes more complex and more remote from subjective experience, confidence in its "objective" character is threatened. The threat is partially realized in the inaccessibility of classified information required to validate aspects of the conventional reality, as well as in the partial consciousness that the mass media and the resources accessible to large organizations are capable of manipulating and "processing" individuals. This tendency is reinforced by the historical record of totalitarian regimes which successfully imposed contrived "conventional realities" on their populations, resulting in genocide, mass political murder, and imperialist war. It is also reinforced by the steady piecemeal flow of observable facts, disturbing details, and miscellaneous data which deny the "common knowledge" of the prevailing conventional reality.

If left unchecked, such tendencies would quickly lead large masses of people to fall back on their subjective experiences; individual and subcultural "reality gaps" would develop which would render political behavior all but unpredictable. What checks these tendencies is, of course, the same massive feature of advanced industrial society which *imposes* the conventional reality on collective consciousness in the first place: the grouping of the bulk of the population into large-scale organizations in such a way that most people (or rather, the income earners in most families) have *stable positions,* however lowly, within at least one of them.

This ensures that the daily lives, life-cycles, and even interclass mobility—where this takes place—of most people are routinized and stabilized. What Berger and Luckmann (*The Social Construction of Reality*), following Alfred Schutz, refer to as the individual's "paramount reality," the "reality of everyday life," is linked, though not (except at the top of the structure) shared, with the reality of the policy-makers of the organization—the "real world" in which they see the organization operating. In corporations, where the production workers are divided by class lines from those higher in the organizational structures, and further more work under highly authoritarian and boring conditions, the trade union representation serves to link the everyday reality of the worker with the "reality" perceived by the union leaders. This in turn either involves a "statesmanlike" appreciation of the difficulties of management or is focused upon the militant determination to use the available institutionalized means of pressure on the latter (strikes, boycotts, favorable legislation and administrative rulings, public relations) so as ultimately to negotiate what is "realistically" the best possible contract—or perhaps, alternatively, *both*. The same principle underlies analogous incidental functions of mass organizations of farmers, small businessmen, and other groups. The point here is not only the well-known "embourgeoisment" of leaders but also the almost unconscious assumptions about the limits of the possible which define the extent of the initial militancy.

The conventional reality not only includes assumptions as to the prevailing distribution of power and the most "effective" and "realistic" means for the discontented to accomplish changes therein; it also prescribes a mentality, or culturally distinctive stance, which links the dealings of the discontented through those who are their agents and representatives with the authorities on the "macro" level ("I think we got the best bill out of this session of Congress that we could reasonably have expected") and with those on the "micro" level ("I think we got the strongest resolution through the Faculty Senate that we could reasonably have expected"). The "realistic" compromise negotiated in bargaining between "hardheaded" but "principled" elites who are "yet serving the common interest" becomes the norm, the ideal, and the point at which all politics culminates, "proving once again the enduring vitality of our free and democratic institutions." The discontented are not necessarily satisfied; but they are normally made to be "realistic."

The conventional reality includes the assumption that salvation for the discontented lies in forming large-scale organizations which, by "aggressively championing their interests" through readily accessible existing institutional channels, will, peacefully, make them "free and equal partners in the pluralistic process of democratic give-and-take." In bourgeois society, the analogous assumption had been that ultimate salvation for the discontented lay in the long-run, unimpeded functioning of the system of self-regulating markets.

With bureaucracy having become the dominant institutional

pattern in society, it acquires the ability to confer social existence upon people by reference to their positions within bureaucracies, or at the very least to their having come in contact with bureaucracies to the extent of having been documented and measured. The organizational present and past of an individual is used as a shorthand guide for locating him in social space and even for establishing a typification of his personality. Galbraith illustrates the impact of this pattern upon casual interaction among corporate executives:

> . . . the large corporation continues to be a symbol of success and achievement in the culture. It endows its members with this prestige; it is obviously better to be a General Motors or Western Electric man then an ordinary unattached citizen. The question automatically asked when two men meet on a plane or in Florida is, "Who are you with?" Until this is known, the individual is a cipher. He cannot be placed in the scheme of things; no one knows how much attention, let alone respect, he deserves or whether he is worthy of any notice at all. If he is with a well-known corporation—a good outfit—he obviously counts.[1]

More important is the reverse of this pattern: the defining out of social existence of people whose way of life does not bring them inside the world of large-scale organizations—and who even evade documentation and measurement:

> I thought I knew what "hard core" meant, until we became involved in this area. I was wrong. Hard core refers not to those without steady jobs, but to those who are not equipped for any job. Not the unemployed, but the unemployable—those who are unable to fill out even a simple job application.
> And it goes much deeper than that. For example, some of these people signed on for job training—with an "X" of course—but failed to show up. And many of those who did report were very late.
> As we registered those who did report, we found that many of them had no social security number, had never been counted in a census, or registered to vote, or belonged to any organization of any kind. In most of the accepted senses, they really didn't even exist.[2]

The "reality of everyday life," from which the conventional reality is generated, is in this society (and in advanced industrial society generally) the hierarchical-authoritarian world of large-scale organizations. Although many of the manifestly brutal and repressive features of this world are removed from sight with increasing affluence (and the less brutal features are liberalized), fundamental inequalities remain. The individual is no longer represented as occupying a quasi-military rank in a regimented chain of command (captains of industry, army of labor), but is depicted instead as a "functioning" component in a smoothly running "system." The definition of sanity in the middle classes becomes the "ability to function." The poor and the disaffected youth are continually urged to "become productive, functioning members of society." Hierarchical authority does not disappear, even when in the guise of a "committee of experts"; it merely appears to "function" also.

Although the inegalitarian "real world" of large organizational life lies at the core of the conventional reality, this "real world" coexists and intermingles with a whole series of *egalitarian* real worlds which are, or have become, hallucinatory. (We can recall William I. Thomas's adage, "If a situation is defined as real, then it will be real in its consequences." We must add, however, that if what has been defined as real is in fact delusory, the real consequences will be psychotic.) The hallucination is that the egalitarian "rights" and "opportunities" involved in the "real world" have the capacity to nullify (either in actuality or potentiality) the manifest inequalities which proceed from the world of large-scale organizations. Objective social hierarchy becomes fantasy equality; both are simultaneously the "real world"; consciousness deals simultaneously with contradictory sets of categories and is thus able to experience freedom and democracy so long as it accepts the need to be realistic and thereby acknowledges in one sphere the legitimacy of power which it denies in the other. The interpretation of social reality in the abstract is always more egalitarian than the behavioral response to social reality in the specific instance.

Among the most important of these hallucinatory dimensions of equality are "rule of law," parliamentarianism, and the "democratic process." The hallucinations here are much more complex and multilayered than what is taught in the seventh-grade "civics" class. Purveyors of the conventional reality always insist that dissidents have the right to organize and go through parliamentary channels; though the same people often vehemently declare, once the dissidents have *been* organized, that the latter have been influenced by "outside agitators."

Those who claim to have the interests of the dissidents at heart—and the dissidents themselves, for everywhere the cry of "We gotta get organized!" is heard—urge the mass organization and the voting bloc as the great solutions. The workers, after all, did it in the thirties. This leads to the "taut-tempered all night negotiating session" where a compromise is "hammered out," and it is "something I think we can live with." It leads to coalitions with other organized interest groups. As Bayard Rustin, that spokesman *par excellence* for the conventional reality during the bourgeois-respectable phase of what was then the "civil rights" movement, was fond of saying during 1964–1965, one progresses "from protest to politics" by forming expedient coalitions with other groups (such as labor and "the churches") on specific issues. The dissidents must refine the arts of "pressure" and "hard bargaining"; the ultimate result to be hoped for is, when viewed abstractly, what Senator Brooke of Massachusetts called "magnificent pluralism."

The closer one comes to the "democratic process," the more one becomes instilled with a hard-bitten cynicism; but the features of parliamentarianism which inspire the cynicism are themselves fully assimilated into the conventional reality. Some of this is just routine: the local organization worker, who does the "real work," otherwise known as the "dirty work," such as composing leaflets, running them off on the mimeograph machine, and distributing them; answering the telephone; raising funds from insensitive outsiders; getting out mailings; and most importantly, "actually going out there into the factory" or "knocking on doors" or "ringing doorbells" and "actually *talking* to the people" or "the membership" or "the voters"—this most definitely is accepted as living in the "real world." The person living there is understandably "pissed at the rest of you who just sit on your asses and talk up a load of bullshit," and righteously expects approval for whatever he may have done between meetings, such as having entered into informal deals, arrangements, and compromises.

Closer to the institutional centers of parliamentarianism, as is automatically assumed by every individual who prides himself on his "realism," it is "unrealistic" to expect anything but a cesspool of iniquity. The sacred precincts of democracy are everywhere assumed to be infested by "machines," clandestine special interests and lobbies, the bribers and the bribed, mafiosi, wheeler-dealers, practitioners and victims of overt and sublimated black-mail, call girls, paunchy alcoholics, entrenched secret masters holding ineffable strings to unknown puppets, and whatever else that is fantasized by the masses, when they silently precede the nouns "politics" and "politician" with the adjective "dirty."

The "inside story" of parliamentary practice is expected to be hard-core pornography; the more shocking the revelations, the more "realistic" it sounds. I once knew a graduate student in political science at Syracuse University who claimed to have ob-tained experience in practical politics as an errand boy for Massa-chusetts state legislators. He said that his duties at a Massachusetts state Democratic convention included delivery to hotel rooms of briefcases stuffed with unmarked bills of small denomination. Then, with the self-satisfied grin of the insider, he exclaimed, "That's what *real* politics is all about—briefcases full of unmarked bills!" In a cultural environment which includes the daily disclo-sures of Drew Pearson and others of his kind, it is difficult to disagree with such an assertion without appearing to be hopelessly naive. And withal, the citizen who looks upon his elected repre-sentatives as a pack of scoundrels and idiots is often apt to regard them with an amused tolerance and accept a romanticized picture of the whole thing as "the great game of politics."

I do not mean to suggest that the "democratic process" is incapable of adjusting to or even initiating "change," or that change is not expected of it. On the contrary, liberalizing reforms are obviously being demanded all the time, and if support is mobilized in the approved and "realistic" fashion, they are ulti-mately enacted ("within realistic limits," of course). What is in practice *not* seriously demanded of the "democratic process" is equality and democracy. The class hierarchy is not leveled either up or down: the top fifth and the bottom fifth of the population receive percentage shares of the national income about the same now as they did twenty-five years ago. Nor is it even remotely con-sidered within the context of the "democratic process" that people should, as a matter of principle, shape their environments to be in accordance with their feelings, rather than themselves be shaped to suit the "functional requirements" of those environments.

"Democracy" remains (as is becoming obvious with the current rapid disintegration of the conventional reality) curiously and compulsively identified with the mere choice between the candidates of the two major parties. This is "freedom"; in this all are "equal." The magical quality of the adherence of the middle class to this notion is perhaps indicated by the confused proliferation of elected governmental units in suburban areas, despite their impotence and irrelevance. Like so many other magical notions in American culture, this one was imposed forcibly on the wretched Vietnamese, who, in September 1967, were made to elect the American-sponsored military regime as their constitutional government (the runner-up candidate was arrested and later sentenced to five years at hard labor.) While subsequent military events demonstrated that the Saigon junta gained no legitimacy among the Vietnamese themselves, the election was taken seriously in official propaganda for the American population at home. It was said to be "a major propaganda victory" that the election "could be held at all," while the half-million or more American troops required for the inadequate protection of the elected, legal, and constitutional regime were to remain lest "the South Vietnamese people lose forever the right to determine their own destiny."

A second great realm of hallucinatory egalitarianism is that of the market economy. The economy is always referred to in public oratory as "private enterprise" or "free enterprise." In public rhetoric, "capitalism" has been treated as mildly obscene, except in such usages as "people's capitalism" (1950s) or "capitalism with a social conscience" (1960s). The fantasy of the self-regulating market theory in the corporate economy has been torn to shreds by Galbraith. But he is not the first, of course. The annihilation of the old "laws" of the market by the corporation, and the simultaneous transformation of property and power relations, was described long before, with varying thoroughness, and at earlier stages of the developmental process (i.e., before the "technostructure" became identifiable), by Schumpeter, Berle and Means, Thurman Arnold, and numerous others. No serious thinker has any further use for the self-regulating market theory as a descriptive model. Yet, as Galbraith himself convincingly demonstrates, the market fantasy is adhered to with blind faith by corporate executives whose behavior in the "real world" of corporate planning has less than nothing to do with what would be anticipated from the theory; while at the same time, professional economists, who claim to be knowledgeable about the behavior of businessmen, analyze the corporate economy as a sort of thoroughly impure market economy rather than as a qualitatively new stage of historical development, and retain a model of human motivation in which the assumptions of the market theory are unchanged. The political advantages for corporate managers and technocrats would not be possible, however, were it not for the fact that the "free market" survives in the "real world" of millions of people (in the middle class, at least), allowing the ideological primitivism of the executive class to be practiced with such ease.

In the old bourgeois culture, the building of a personal fortune out of a small business and next to no capital was the cultural ideal—the "American Dream." The ability to do this required "individual initiative," "enterprise," and "independence." Such at least was the imagery. The ideal personality supposedly displayed a rigid compartmentalization between subjective satisfaction and economic rationality. The culture hero could be asocial to the point of anarchic violence; once risen to a position of authority, he could be legitimately merciless toward weaker competitors, while knowing "how to handle the men" and put down crackpots and troublemakers, and being quick to defend the honor of women. The generalized fulfillment of such ideals, however, would soon have made social organization impossible. In any case, the bureaucratization of the economy rendered the more grandiose forms of such fulfillment obsolete.

The bureaucratic sublimation of the ideals of bourgeois mythology and the American Dream were Equality of Opportunity and Success. The ambitious man climbed to the top (or part of the way up) of already existing structures, instead of creating entirely new structures after the manner of the vanished mythological heroes of the economic frontier. But the failure to be "independent" could be made to weigh guiltily on those who were merely pursuing careers or working at jobs. For the organization middle class, the ideal of "independence" added a special compulsiveness to the desire for success; yet since success depended upon conformity to the functional requirements of the organization, there appeared that strange drivenness in adjustment that was remarked upon by the social critics of the 1950s. There was the guilty knowledge that the career in the large organization was itself a species of selling out; this must have added a special dimension to the status anxieties that were discussed so widely. Farther down the class hierarchy, many production workers sustained themselves at this time with fantasies of their own farms or small businesses (see Eli Chinoy, *Automobile Workers and the American Dream*). At the top, those businessmen who kept the purity of the old bourgeois faith have long bemoaned the characterological decadence made inevitable by the very same large-scale organizations which some of them helped to create. Apropos of a discussion of the process by which capitalism destroys its own values, Michael Harrington notes:

> In the thirties, Russell Leffingwell of Morgan's told an investigating committee, "The growth of corporate enterprise has been drying up individual independence and initiative. . . . We are becoming a nation of hired men. Hired by great aggregates of capital." [3]

And in the present day, Barry Goldwater honors the legend of the bare-knuckled capitalism of the desert frontier at the expense of more conventional Republicans "in their good gray business suits."

Small business, though marginal to the functioning of capitalism, is fundamental to its legitimacy. For those who are relatively content with existing institutional arrangements, there must at least be a moderately compulsive urge to avoid contemplation of the circumstances perceived by Harrington which lead him to observe:

> Practically every ethical, moral, and cultural justification for the capitalist system has now been destroyed by capitalism. The idyll of the free market, risktaking, inventiveness, the social virtue of making money, all these have been abolished by the very success of capitalism itself. [4]

For those retaining the will to believe, the only possible living proof of the enduring value of the bourgeois ethos must be the small businessman. In fantasy there is projected onto him all the impossibilities and irrelevances of the American Dream. To actually state the full implications of the American Dream in public today would be idiotic. Barry Goldwater could nevertheless say in a campaign speech in front of a Colgate toothpaste factory in Indiana in 1964 that, "We could have a hundred Colgates. A thousand Colgates!" He neglected to indicate where to find the required quantity of additional teeth.

The explicit manipulative use of the myth of the small businessman to legitimize the giant corporation may be observed in a two-page color advertisement placed in national magazines during the summer of 1968 by the Shell Oil Company. The picture shows a mob of Shell employees occupying various stations in life, including what has become the *de rigueur* token black executive in three-piece gray flannel suit and carrying a gray-green attaché case. There is also a black proletarian in uniform, as well as an inconspicuous old black lady in the back row. The entire assemblage nevertheless conveys the impression of a display of White Power. The text of the advertisement:

> If you don't want to work for a big corporation, have a big corporation work for you.
>
> Being your own boss is a pretty good setup. You make the decisions, set the goals, get the profits. But there's one thing better.
>
> Being your own boss and having a three-billion-dollar corporation behind you. Like Shell. A Shell dealer has more people working for him than just his manager, attendants and mechanics. Before he opens, he has the services of a talented architect. He has chemical and petroleum engineers constantly improving on the products he sells.
>
> He has a staff of consultants available to him, to advise him on how to operate more efficiently. To help create advertising for him. To offer him useful merchandising ideas and materials. Shell advisors can help a dealer with his special accounting problems. His financing. Even his public speaking.
>
> But there's an obligation that goes with being a successful businessman. Shell dealers are called on to help in various local community projects. In safety drives. In clean-up programs. Sometimes in town planning. They serve as councilmen, aldermen, selectmen—even mayors.
>
> Why does a Shell dealer work hard for the community? Because it's not just a place to do business.
>
> It's where he makes his home.

As I have already said, and as should be obvious even from the above text, the franchised dealer is little more than a trained civil servant. Yet he is expected to fantasize himself as an independent businessman of bygone days. I now leave it to the imagination of the reader to fantasize about the problem of maintaining the conventional reality of all those Shell people holding local office, the great bulk of them doubtless being incensed over high taxes and "big government reaching like an octopus into every nook and cranny of this nation."

The semiegalitarian principle of careers open to talent overlays the older cultural substratum of the American Dream, with the result that the meaning of "opportunity" has become repressively and unduly constricted to imply "economic opportunity": the ascent to an executive position within the corporation or to prominence in the profession, together with the insistent accumulation of personal wealth and consumer goods as tokens of achievement. "Unduly constrictive" refers to the fact that the meaning of "opportunity" has failed to be broadened to include other values to a degree commensurate with the growth of the national wealth.

With the sustained and rising affluence of the middle class in the 1950s, the organizationally allowed career lines were accepted by trained and educated youth only as a result—or as a by-product—of the repressive atmosphere of McCarthyism and the height of the Cold War. This produced the youth culture of cynical and complacent conformity called the "silent generation."

Following the lifting of political and cultural repression during 1958–1962, the consequences of the failure to gradually redefine "opportunity" became dramatically apparent in very short order as masses of middle-class youth reacted with disgust to the spectacle of available careers in existing institutions. This reaction is totalistic in that all existing institutions are seen as in need of an overhaul before they become acceptable environments; failing that, any job taken with any objective other than securing the means of subsistence, or with any sense of loyalty to the organization, represents a species of selling out. The fact that many *do* begin their careers may be less relevant than the joke with which this is announced: "I just joined the system—I got a job." It is not really a joke. As a hippie ideologist put it:

> The world needs less specialists in force and more generalists in love. . . .
>
> Politics, administration, bureaucracy, are concerned primarily with POWER, that is, the coercion of individuals.
>
> Who would want to coerce individuals eight hours a day when he could be walking in the woods, fucking, painting, making a useful and artistic object, growing beautiful food, making music, thinking, writing (even), talking to friends, helping cure the sick, watching movies, reading, teaching the beautiful young and there-

fore learning from the beautiful young (plenty of power-mad sad people here too) etc., etc., etc?
WHO WANTS TO ORDER ANYBODY TO DO ANYTHING?

Politicians, the state, the total body politic, the repressive and coercive forces, the lackeys of the bourgeoisie, the big and petty bureaucrats, the bad teachers, sadistic cops, soldiers trained to kill, mechanistic physicians, miserable inhuman designers of bureaucratic antihuman things, the unanswerable foremen, the dictator-bosses, the autocratic parents determined their children shall grow up as miserable as they are etc., etc., etc. THAT'S WHO.

So that the best shun power—they want to play and to love—not to intimidate and to interfere and to control.

Love is the freedom of the beloved.

Since the most sick, the most unhappy, the meanest, the most deprived, the most perceptually distorted, and the most frustrated, are those who seek power—the power structure is corrupt—the power creates sickness, the power fucks up what it was intended to heal, the power creates war, death; it tolerates poverty, arrests people, imprisons them, destroys foreign cultures physically and emotionally, turns—via the mass media—its own citizens into zombies who attack whatever is pointed out to them.[5]

Redefining "opportunity" at this stage of the game really looks like a leap into the unknown. Consider now that the reference in the passage quoted above to "the autocratic parents determined their children shall grow up as miserable as they are," as far as the readers of this publication (average age nineteen) are concerned, might well refer to all parents. Such youth experience their parents as believers in economic opportunity. And economic opportunity (and on a deeper level, the American Dream, of which it is but the bureaucratic sublimation) is understood to be a great and wondrous *egalitarian possibility*. We must at some point ask ourselves whether we seek to impose an Office of Economic Opportunity upon the black lower class in order to escape having to redefine "opportunity" for ourselves. It is the great opening in the closed system for the youth with ambition, talent, and education, or so it is engraved in the conventional reality. ("We're giving you a college education, and we *couldn't afford* to go to college when we wanted to. . . . *Of course* we love you—look at all the things we gave you.") When the youth ignores this egalitarian possibility, regards it as bureaucratic servitude, and refuses to accept what he regards as senseless repression associated with getting his education and pursuing his career, he is accused of "throwing his life away."

The egalitarian fantasies of the consumer experiencing the free market in his consumer choices are almost too obvious to mention. These fantasies only make him more completely supine before the repressive force of advertising. On the other hand, he can enter the market freely to consume himself into equality with the Joneses.

Still another hallucinatory, egalitarian dimension of the conventional reality is the tribal myth of the equality of all armed Anglo-Saxon white men. Accordingly, one's shootin' iron used to be affectionately referred to as an "equalizer." American society was almost unique in its democratization of the ownership of firearms; this may have been largely responsible for the broad streak of anarchic violence which runs through the culture. Americans persecute dissidents by means of the lynch mob rather than the state (though the latter has been used often enough); they have rarely rebelled for political ends, but they commit many private murders. "Property," especially that in land, is intensely tinged with violent meanings. Ownership of property, such as land in a suburban housing subdivision, is a mark of personal power, as well as of sexual potency. The property owner is a real *man* and he feels damn well free to sell to any white man he chooses. For the state to regulate his property, and to confiscate his weapon, would be an act of castration. He requires both to protect his women against the incursions of criminal elements and minority races.

This dimension of the culture is permitted to survive side by side with the dimension involving the rule of law and parliamentarianism; if cultural contradictions become too glaring, violent urges can always be projected onto dissidents and powerless groups. Both dimensions are intermingled with "free-market" fantasies in the worship of the pioneer-entrepreneur, who staked out a fortune where "the only law was the law of the gun," by the white middle and working classes whose political representatives react to the dissidence of the black population with bellicose oratory about "respect for law and order," while promising "necessary reforms to secure economic opportunity through the orderly channels of the democratic process."

Paragons of bourgeois respectability or bureaucratic mediocrity still preach "rugged individualism" at each other. The Right still continues to combine opposition to federal regulation of both business and firearms with dire warnings of the castrating tendencies of "the bloated centralizing bureaucracy reaching into the private lives of individuals"—while supporting wiretapping and terroristic searches and seizures by the police. In the conventional reality all these weird cultural contradictions are reconciled.

To hallucinate equality, freedom, openness, and individualism, where objectively there is—to an irrational degree, in light of the existing development of productive facilities—hierarchy, brutality, constriction in personal and social behavior, and standardization is to support the failure to conceive of social progress beyond technological change and economic growth. As a young artist recently wrote in a Boston "underground" newspaper, "Man tends to realize the limits of his imagination and call it progress." [6]

Karl Polanyi held that only in very recent history did the strictly economic sphere come to be separated out of the total context of social life. The bourgeois social order of the nineteenth century, in which social life was ruthlessly submerged by the requirements of the self-regulating market economy, represented an extreme in the dissociation of economy and society, though society, to protect itself from dissolution, had to take steps to reabsorb the economy back into itself. Concern with economic problems remained uppermost because of the need for accumulation of disposable surplus to press the industrialization process to its conclusion. But with this point having been reached, personal freedom

> should be upheld at all cost—even that of efficiency in production, economy in consumption or rationality in administration. An industrial society can afford to be free.
> The passing of market-economy can become the beginning of an era of unprecedented freedom. Juridical and actual freedom can be made wider and more general than ever before; regulation and control can achieve freedom not only for the few, but for all. Freedom not as an appurtenance of privilege, tainted at the source, but as a prescriptive right extending far beyond the narrow confines of the political sphere into the intimate organization of society itself. Thus will old freedoms and civic rights be added to the fund of new freedom generated by the leisure and security that industrial society offers to all. Such a society can afford to be both just and free.[7]

Polanyi wrote that in 1944, having in mind the possibilities of the Welfare State. But such hopes were aborted; we now have a much richer society that is neither just nor free.

A hangover of bourgeois society and culture is the Market-Scarcity Principle. It assumes the insufficiency of things-in-general; it implies the submission of the individual to the repressive authority of the organizers of production in order to continue the receipt of a limited share in the allocation of scarce goods. At its logical conclusion it implies that he who does not work shall starve —and even *deserves* to starve; in any case, the protection of such people from the possibility of starvation because of charitable inclinations or sentimental pity is unscientific, since it threatens the society as a whole with economic ruin. (During the period of unambiguous acceptance of bourgeois ideology, the latter notion could be used to rationalize genocide, as during the Irish potato famine.) More usually (even though people still starve to death in the United States today, in Mississippi and Alabama), the practical application becomes the denial of social existence to people defined as not "productive"; they are subjected to systematic degradation.

Under the Welfare State, this cultural logic is challenged and the effort is made to replace it with a cultural principle under which all those who happen to be alive are understood to have the right to live without the denial of social existence. Recent American history suggests that this could have been done briefly only because, during the Great Depression, the economy was obviously collapsing; industrial capitalism was a self-evident failure; large sections of the semiskilled and skilled working classes and even the lower middle classes had been forcibly expelled from the "labor market." With the return of abundance and previously undreamed of heights of prosperity, the cultural principle underlying the Welfare State has been subjected to systematic erosion and even obliteration. Not even something as basic as the removal of medical care as a matter of principle from the cultural category of consumer goods purchased in the marketplace has yet become established as part of the conventional reality.

When the governor of New York introduced his "Medicaid" program (free medical care for the "medically indigent" with an upper income limit of $6,000 per year) in 1966, a Syracuse, New York, newspaper denounced the scheme as "wildly socialistic";

subsequent reactionary pressure obtained extensive limitations and reductions in the scope and coverage of the plan. Poor, and in particular black, citizens requiring the services of free medical clinics find themselves subjected to hours of waiting in emergency rooms; are treated as objects for the education of medical students; and wind up at the bottom of the three-class (private-semiprivate-ward) stratification of the quality of hospital care. If the life expectancy of black people in New York City is ten years less than that for whites, the conventional reality does not include this under the heading of inequality. The "respectable" citizen draws an altogether different conclusion. For instance: a graduate student at Syracuse University had an attack of a recurrent intestinal disease while she was visiting a friend in Washington, D.C. The friend called the free emergency ambulance service. The sadistic ambulance attendants refused to let her lie down during the trip to the hospital. At the free public hospital, the treatment was of the same humiliating order. Recounting the experience later, she drew the "realistic" conclusion: "I'm never again going to be in a situation where I can't afford to be sick."

One would expect that the Scarcity Principle would dissolve with the increase in material abundance. This has failed to occur among people of the older generations because of memories of extreme objective scarcity such as the Great Depression, because of the continuing creation of new needs and their inculcation by the mass media, and because of the status anxieties in which consumer goods and other indications of wealth or "success" serve as objective indices of respectability. The unambiguous distinction between Success and Failure is perhaps most fundamental in sustaining these status anxieties; and in order for the concept of Success to retain its full repressive force and mystique, it is necessary that there be an aggregation of readily identifiable, actual, walking, talking Failures.

In this we may perceive the most powerful motive underlying the cultural tendency to define poverty as a *disease* rather than as an absence of wealth—specifically money. (If someone really desires to eliminate the culture of poverty and "break the cycle of dependency," I suggest that some "policy maker" try the following pilot program: simply distribute to every family unit and unattached individual in, say, Central Harlem an annual income of

$8,000, *absolutely guaranteed against termination for any reason,* including imprisonment. Then stand back and watch the "culture of poverty" disappear.) Those whom the economy casts out as perfectly useless must be subjected to continual indoctrination and hallucinatory advice and help, in the hope that they will become "productive, useful citizens." Failing this, it is necessary to humiliate them and deny them social existence, for those above them in the social scale, who tolerate being subjected to extravagant repression in return for being considered marginally useful and productive, would never countenance the idea that "society owes anybody a living." One detects in this the desire in each social substratum to appear more respectable and productive than the group immediately below, such that the entire range of conventional restrictions on personal appearance and expression is held in place, though subject to a process of gradual liberalization as required for the most efficient organization of production and the most effective manipulation of consumption.

The liberalization of the productive side is to some extent encouraged by the subjectivizing impact of the mass culture, which is the vehicle for the maintenance of the level of consumption. You do not sell a soft drink as "the mad mad mad mad cola" or impute orgasmic properties to beer by having a scantily clad young woman appear on the tube and, with a wink and an inviting motion of the index finger, sing "live the Genesee moment . . . come along with me," or sell an Oldsmobile as a rejuvenation machine ("young it up for real in a youngmobile")—you do not, in the course of spending $15 billion a year on advertising, avoid a cumulative effect even on those who foot the bill. Employees might even be required to personify the relaxed company "image" established through advertising (though this would itself be repressive).

A most significant example of the wave of the immediate present is the spreading vogue of "sensitivity training," as developed by the psychologist Carl Rogers. Not surprisingly, this liberalizing device is spreading fastest among managements in advanced technology industries, where the extreme specialization and technological sophistication of the employees exists in profound contradiction to the subjectivizing influence of the mass culture, not to mention the complexity of consciousness to be expected in highly intelligent and well-educated people. A recent issue of *Look* magazine proclaims a "New Era In Industry: It's OK to Cry in the Office." [8] But the lead into the article, by *Look* Senior Editor John Poppy, makes it perfectly clear that it is efficiency in production which is the driving force behind this liberalization; one does not *start* with any selfless desire to see whole people encounter each other as whole people:

> A California aerospace contractor is one of the hundreds of companies learning that honestly shared emotions help get the work done better.[9]

Poppy describes the exploitation of "sensitivity training" within TRW Systems Group (a subdivision of the conglomerate giant TRW Inc.), a rapidly growing war-and-space contractor with 16,500 employees at last count. It must be objectively considered as an accomplice to some of the most monstrous evil going on in the world today ("Since the day it started planning the Air Force's Minuteman ICBM network in 1954, TRW Systems has been making money along the frontier of technology.");[10] a sort of American DEGESCH (German Vermin-Exterminating Corporation, which manufactured the Zyklon B for Auschwitz; it was a subsidiary of I. G. Farben). If this fact is borne in mind, the article becomes incredibly fascinating. *For this organization liberalizes itself and turns its employees into "better human beings" so that they can function more efficiently in contributing to the manufacture of death.*

Poppy spells out management's logic:

> The company, even more than most, runs on intricate teamwork. A "system" comprises all the different parts—switches, circuits, valves, sensors—making a thing operate. That includes people. A TRW engineer is no hermit inventor cooped up behind barbed wire. He moves among other specialists, many of them plugged into his daily job. He reports to a project manager, collaborates with scientists, needs support from administrators, feeds work to production-line assemblers and has to make his task— designing an antenna, say—mesh with everyone else's.
> . . . What if the antenna engineer hit a snag in his calculations but refused to confess the trouble for fear that it would damage his reputation and chances for promotion? What if he spent a lot of energy defending a mistake once it came to light? What if he felt resentment toward a colleague who offered help? Obviously, the man would suffer. So would the company.

> But the competitive culture of most organizations teaches just
> that sort of behavior. Human hang-ups not only make people
> miserable; they contaminate the work.[11]

As if the work itself were not something that did not contaminate
all who touched it. But the TRW personnel managers increase
efficiency (" 'We have very few technical problems,' says an
industrial engineer, 'just people problems.' ") by including in its
Career Development program—headed by a Ph.D. in anthropology
—a Leadership Development Laboratory, including three days of
sensitivity training. Poppy follows thirty-six men into this process;
they are typical technostructure specimens ("scientists, engineers,
managers, some with Ph.D.s"). The most obvious motive for participation in the "sensitivity training" is career advancement within
the organization ("It's going to be a big waste of time, some
thought. But the word was out in the company: Try it. So they
would try it."). The course begins:

> Pinning on nametags—first name only, no indication of rank
> or job—they heard some ground rules. "While you're here, try to
> be absolutely honest," said one of the five "trainers" from the
> TRW personnel department on hand to help if needed. "Level
> with each other. Let the people in your group share what you
> *feel* from the gut. Second, stay in the here and now. Don't be
> distracted by the past or future; focus on what's happening right
> here at this moment. Third, no physical violence." [12]

What is ominous here is that this is an indication of the desire to
establish a controlled freak-out in which it is ensured that minds
are blown only so far and no farther. The emotions can be exposed,
but in a direction which is "functional" for the organization. It is
not to be contemplated that somebody will recognize that he hates
somebody else—and be permitted to let it go at that. Least of all
is it contemplated that valuable specialists will have their minds so
far blown that they will drop out of the organization altogether,
possibly as a result of having made some sort of higher conceptual
connection between the petty repressions and brutalities of daily
life, on the one hand, and the objective uses of the products which
they help to manufacture on the other. The achievement of such
control is assisted by the insistence that the participants concen-
trate on the "here and now" to the exclusion of discussion of company life ("the participants have to build a social system, from
scratch, inside the room" [13]); the impression is conveyed that the

subjective life operates without any relevance at all to the social order which shaped it to begin with.

The participants split into three groups.

> In Group One, the eyes all turned to Dr. George Lehner, "outside" consultant for this lab. Lehner, a seal-sleek, soft-spoken UCLA psychology professor, is one of nine consultants on human behavior retained year-round by TRW Systems. He was a resource for the group, not a controller, he said, but just to get things started, how about sitting in a circle? "Now, pick someone across from you. How do you react to him? How do you feel about being here?" [14]

The participants quickly recognize manipulative motives in each other and in the situation as a whole.

> Bert, a balding production foreman who kept a suit jacket buttoned over his sport shirt, looked around quickly to see if anyone else was ready, then announced: "I think we can all get a lot out of this. I hope to learn some new methods for being an understanding manager and motivating workers. . . ."
>
> "Methods? You mean like tricks?" The question came from Matt, Irish and aggressive. His voice was sharp. He squinted at Lehner. "That bothers me. He sounds so cold-blooded. . . ."
>
> "Don't tell *me*, Matt," Lehner said. "Say it to Bert."
>
> Matt did. Bert shrugged. Someone filled the silence with another remark. Around the circle went comments carefully phrased as feelings without revealing much feeling, until David, younger than most of the group, said, "You all came up with something so fast, I feel as if everyone is obeying an *order* to talk. Do we have to be so obedient? I don't feel ready yet. I'll wait." [15]

But antagonisms and irritations are skillfully intensified *between* and *among* the participants, forestalling the possibility that any hostility might crystallize or be focused upon the organization or the "training" situation itself. The participants come to use the solidarity of the organization as a club with which to smash each other open:

> Matt bored in with a wide-eyed stare into Chris's eyes: "Yes, I find you just as unpleasant to deal with here as back at Space Park. You come on so strong that I give you a fast answer to get you out of my office—not always the best answer, either, just the fastest."
>
> Chris paused, "Why didn't you tell me that two years ago?"
>
> Lehner intervened, gently: "Why put the burden on him, Chris?"
>
> "Listen, I get impatient with people when they don't react as

fast as they should," Chris said. "I don't have time to wet-nurse everyone."

"But that probably makes you less efficient," David sweated with the effort of making himself face Chris, two feet away. "You muddy up people's reactions when you make them resent you. I'm mad right now, for instance, so I'm probably not functioning too well." [16]

Some of the remarks made by Dr. Lehner the next morning further the effort to exploit the increased sensitivity to intensify the smoothly functioning character of the organizational machine. Dr. Lehner also reveals the concern of management—in the interests of efficiency—with eliminating the more crippling individual pathologies deriving from the Success ethic, without, however, eliminating the Success ethic itself:

". . . we don't complain about fulfilling the systems of a machine —a car, for instance. We make sure we have air in the tires, oil in the engine, water in the radiator, gas in the tank . . . but how much do we do about fulfilling the needs of this ambulatory system, the human being? I'd feel very uncomfortable if I had to drive my car with all the gauges taped over. Shouldn't we feel uncomfortable if we can't read our own gauges?

"Many of us get tremendous kicks from taking a set of data, manipulating it and solving a problem. Yet without satisfaction on the feeling level, technical productivity is useless to us. We already know one of you who has advanced steadily in the company, performs his job so well that he is praised by his superiors, but feels inside like a failure. This man can't enjoy any of his triumphs. . . ."

Group One carefully avoided looking around at Bruce. . . .

". . . Try for a win-win situation. If a man brings you a set of plans and you want to modify them, don't just throw them down and overlay your own ideas. That would be win-lose—you win at the other man's expense. Stay with him. *Listen to him.* Try to make yourself understood without smothering him. You can still change the plans and you both win. You are both satisfied at the feeling level." [17]

But the next day, with everybody's defenses starting to crumble, young David seems to teeter on the brink of a truly historic moment in the missile industry:

"I want to be a good man," he said, choosing words slowly. "That means changing the world, making it a less wasteful place. I can't just rattle through my job, take the money, go home and tune out. . . ." Pause. Words began to spill faster. "You know why what we're doing in this room is important? Think of all the stopped-up energy we can release in here once we quit using up our strength straining against each other, or hiding inside. Once we learn to run free with it, there's no limit to what we might do. . . . And why can't it happen out there? . . .

"I've had some glimpses . . . people who were wide open, moving together . . . it's like being in a really good kind of love. But most of the time, watching what people do to themselves breaks your heart. . . . It breaks your heart. . . .

"Sometimes you'd think everybody is crazy. . . ." He stared at the light of the window: ". . . flinging incredible amounts of energy around, everywhere you look . . . wasted. We do such violence to each other. We're fighting wars . . . race, we're fighting each other, scaring children at school, scaring them at home. . . . Nobody could do any of it if they weren't so locked up inside of themselves, out of touch with the people they hurt. God, I hate all that violence. . . ." [18]

But instead of carrying this train of thought to its catastrophic (for company policy) conclusion, David continues in a direction which under the circumstances must be considered a cop-out: he blurts out a story of how he once almost murdered his wife for no particular reason. The group understands and tenderly supports him. Poor David! An explosion of universal love which will transform the world and abolish war and violence (bad for TRW business) is transformed into a happier way to make missiles.

To complete the picture, Poppy interviews Sheldon A. Davis, "Vice-President for industrial (that is, employee) relations." Davis looks tough ("Tall and burly, mournful of mien under a gray-flecked crew-cut") and talks tough:

> Disturbed by the "soft, mushy, sweetness-and-light impressions" that many people connect with sensitivity training, Davis points out that TRW's objectives are tough: "In dealing with one another we will be open, direct, explicit. Our feelings will be available to one another, and we will try to problem-solve rather than be defensive." The aim is "a more effective, efficient, problem-solving organization." [19]

In TRW, the Leadership Development Laboratory is only "basic training." What is acquired there is sustained in the "job family," consisting of a supervisor and his subordinates.

It is a comforting thought that American instruments of mass death are manufactured with so much "sensitivity." Maybe this is an example of what Herbert Marcuse meant when he said that "these possibilities are gradually being realized through means and institutions which cancel their liberating potential, and this process affects not only the means but also the ends." [20] And maybe it is something even worse.

CHAPTER 5

A Few Words About Total Systems

Social theorists deal in monstrous visions of self-contained total-ism; they share the basic assumption of the omnipotence of the "system" but differ on the question of whether it is fit to live in. Talcott Parsons is on the Right; his Social System tends toward "integration" and "equilibrium" as it keeps on "functioning"—for the purposes of its own ("system goals," of which "economic growth" is "paramount") that for mere humans to try to alter would be childish folly. Whatever exists is functional (good) pro-vided it has been around long enough to merit the benefit of the doubt as to its having arisen through structural and functional differentiation. "Deviance" of whatever kind becomes incorporated as it somehow becomes functional (if only reinforcing the "inte-gration" of everything else); otherwise it is "dysfunctional" (bad) and will (should) be eliminated by those endowed with "legiti-macy" and "loyalty" (or it will subsist in some dark corner because it is "functionally irrelevant"—useless, harmless, or trivial).

John Kenneth Galbraith is in the Center. He has come to realize that the countervailing powers at the most relevant level fail to countervail but instead coalesce and combine; the "new industrial state" is a higher unity of great corporations, a state that subsidizes and regulates dependent trade unions, and mass media through which new needs are implanted in the consumers. Galbraith insists that the main features of the "new industrial state" are necessary if the economy is to continue to deliver the goods on the present (or a greater) scale—to consumers who never really placed the order in the first place. Galbraith retains an attitude of aristocratic contempt for the values and some of the material consequences of the "industrial system"; but his theory has no place for the scruffy dissidence of the black lower classes and sections of middle-class youth. While the poor had best practice "cultural accommodation to the needs of the industrial system," a gentlemanly and conventionally organized dissidence on aesthetic and moral issues can be expected to be mounted by the comfortable and sophisticated—and, of course, white—academic middle class ("the educational and scientific estate"). Galbraith himself gives several excellent reasons for believing that political action dominated by this group would be doomed to ineffectuality and incorporation. Yet he is either awaiting the Messiah or fatuously describing himself when he claims:

> . . . it is possible that the educational and scientific estate requires only a strongly creative political hand to become a decisive instrument of political power.[1]

We know that the academic middle class remained under the spell of the rightist purges and intimidation of the 1950s until subjected to the countercoercive pressure of the students, who have consistently dragged the professoriate along in their wake. In the final chapter of *The New Industrial State,* Galbraith reflects that aspect of the conventional reality which associates political impact exclusively with the "effectiveness" of formal organization guided by the controlling hand of hierarchical authority:

> This is written at a time [1966–1967] of much rather incoherent and unfocused dissent by younger people. Much of this dissent reflects a dissatisfaction with the goals so self-confidently asserted by the industrial system and its spokesmen. It will be highly responsive to leadership. It will be unfocused and ineffective unless this leadership is supplied.[2]

As I will demonstrate later, the dissidence of the youth derives its impact from these very qualities of being "incoherent" and "unfocused." Nor are the youth (at least the youth I have in mind) responsive to leadership, even from among themselves. But Galbraith was writing before the events at Columbia University which began on April 23, 1968; perhaps more importantly, he was writing before April-May 1968, when about a dozen sociology students at the University of Nanterre, outside Paris, set in motion a train of events which freaked out an entire nation.

Herbert Marcuse may by universal accord be assigned to the Left; but the comprehensive disgust and hostility which he manifests toward advanced industrial society as a totally organized apparatus of domination is equaled only by the despair that his theories are almost calculated to inspire in the reader. Not only does he see the great bureaucratic organizations of outwardly pluralistic welfare-state capitalism as tending to fuse into a subtle form of totalitarianism; the system also generates a culture which inhibits the development of consciousness of the true extent of repression and authoritarian manipulation, and an understanding of the comprehensively totalitarian features of the system. It is impossible for thought to escape contamination with the assumptions that underlie the structure and behavior of existing institutions. Language and philosophy become devices whereby man is made to avoid becoming conscious of the existence of the possibility of his own liberation; the intellectual tools for the formulation of a comprehensive negation of the existing order are not permitted to exist. Sex, "tolerance" as a generalized principle, freedoms of press and speech, as well as other civil liberties—all these have their repressive and manipulative aspects: "repressive desublimation" prevents true instinctual liberation, while "Under the rule of a repressive whole, liberty can be made into a powerful instrument of domination." And furthermore,

> . . . domination—in the guise of affluence and liberty—extends to all spheres of private and public existence, integrates all authentic opposition, absorbs all alternatives. Technological rationality reveals its political character as it becomes the great vehicle of better domination, creating a truly totalitarian universe in which society and nature, mind and body are kept in a state of permanent mobilization for the defense of this universe.[3]

The inevitable—and depressing—conclusions which Marcuse had to draw from his own theoretical position are: First, since the totalitarian system, by manipulating and mobilizing the consciousness of practically everyone to secure complete acceptance and legitimation of itself, prevents the formulation of alternatives to itself, the population does not in any large numbers desire its own liberation; therefore it is not possible to have even the foggiest notion of the forms and contents, structure and governance, and cultural values and modal personality that would prevail in the liberated society. Second, the chances are that liberation will be prevented altogether and that we will get liberalization on the system's own terms. Third, opposition to a totalitarian system must itself be total; but this is likely to appear to all sound and realistic thinkers as hilarious, impractical, or quixotic. Fourth, in order to attack the totalitarian system at any specific point, it is apparently necessary to organize politically and in a formal fashion in order to participate in the legislative struggle; but this violates the principle of total opposition and runs the risk of incorporation. Fifth (unstated), it's no use:

> The critical theory of society, was, at the time of its origin, confronted with the presence of real forces (objective and subjective) *in* the established society which moved (or could be guided to move) toward more rational and freer institutions by abolishing the existing ones which had become obstacles to progress. These were the empirical grounds on which the theory was erected, and from these empirical grounds derived the idea of the liberation of *inherent* possibilities—the development, otherwise blocked and distorted, of material and intellectual productivity, faculties, and needs. Without the demonstration of such forces, the critique of society would still be valid and rational, but it would be incapable of translating its rationality into terms of historical practice. The conclusion? "Liberation of inherent possibilities" no longer adequately expresses the historical alternative.
>
> The enchained possibilities of advanced industrial societies . . . are gradually being realized through means and institutions which cancel their liberating potential, and this process affects not only the means but also the ends. The instruments of productivity and progress, organized into a totalitarian system, determine not only the actual but also the possible utilizations.
>
> At its most advanced stage, domination functions as administration, and in the overdeveloped areas of mass consumption, the administered life becomes the good life of the whole, in the defense of which the opposites are united. This is the pure form of domination. Conversely, its negation appears to be the pure form of negation. All content seems reduced to the one abstract de-

mand for the end of domination—the only truly revolutionary exigency, and the event that would validate the achievements of industrial civilization. In the face of its efficient denial by the established system, this negation appears in the politically impotent form of the "absolute refusal"—a refusal whch seems the more unreasonable the more the established system develops its productivity and alleviates the burden of life. . . .

. . . The totalitarian tendencies of the one-dimensional society render the traditional ways and means of protest ineffective—perhaps even dangerous because they preserve the illusion of popular sovereignty. This illusion contains some truth: "the people," previously the ferment of social change, have "moved up" to become the ferment of social cohesion. Here rather than in the redistribution of wealth and equalization of classes is the new stratification characteristic of advanced industrial society.[4]

Superficially, Marcuse and Parsons would seem to have little in common beyond Teutonicized English prose and failures in the area of naturalistic description. But Marcuse has apparently theorized about an antisystem that is the mirror image of Parsons' Social System. In both theories the system is all embracing, total, and omnipotent. It certainly gets inside the head: in Parsons' version, the personality system replicates the values of the social system as a whole as transmitted by means of the socialization process; it is "integrated with" the social system additionally in being adapted to assorted role behaviors and normative patterns imposed from without. This becomes for Marcuse totalitarian domination, regimentation, control, and the imposition of one-dimensional modes of thought upon the individual. Both versions of the system are pretty much "conflict-free"; for Parsons, this would be an anticipated outcome of a high degree of societal integration (a good thing), while Marcuse excoriates what he perceives as an overwhelming yet subtle *Gleichschaltung*. In both versions the system functions mindlessly, pursuing its primary objective of increasing material abundance with higher productivity and more advanced technology; to this end it does whatever is feasible to facilitate its own functioning (or domination). In both theories, as I have already noted, major substantive, consciously directed, organized efforts at change are not of much use; for Parsons, the system always tends to reestablish equilibrium anyway, while the electoral process is a "rite" which serves primarily to reintegrate loyalties in the political system, with the same constellation of forces remaining in power—with minor modifications—no matter who is elected; for Marcuse, the traditional channels of organized political change are ineffectual at best and carry with them the danger of the incorporation into the system of any enduring formally organized hierarchical structure.

The family resemblance in the assumption in each theory of absolute totalism in the social order ends, of course, most prominently with the issue of coercion. Parsons holds that where the more obvious forms of suppression are not used, coercion is not present and is not necessary: people get born, are socialized, perform their role behaviors, and die; there is nothing going on for the social theorist to get *emotional* about. Marcuse maintains that there is total coercion, to which the theorist must respond with total hostility: people get forcibly expelled from the womb, are corrupted by one-dimensional thought, lead meaningless lives as tools of a totalitarian system, and are finally killed—most often by diseases over which they have no control.

It is not surprising that one theory should have found favor with a coterie of sociologists during a period of compulsive national self-reassurance presided over by Dwight D. Eisenhower to what appeared to be the mild satisfaction of nearly everybody; nor is it surprising that Marcuse has grown in popularity among other coteries of sociologists who are repelled by the smugness of the first group and who are surprised by growing national crises; nor is it very surprising that both have been ignored by most American sociologists, who find theories on this level of abstraction to be meaningless gibberish unrelated to doing "meaningful" research in the "real" world.

What is surprising at first glance is that Marcuse should have become an international teen-age idol. By reluctantly accepting the features of the conventional reality dealing with the possible means for effecting political change, he condemns dissidents to either howling in the wilderness or engaging in activities which they know in advance are meaningless. Part of the answer is unwittingly given by a leftist academic who finds Marcuse's totalist vision too impractical and unrealistic:

> But the real help we need is not in giving nightmares an intellectual structure. It is in beginning to answer questions about the politics of the "totalizing" and "post-totalized" society.[5]

The youth to whom Marcuse appeals, however, want the nightmare much more than the intellectual structure. Marcuse's totalist theory reinforces their inclination to regard the total system as irremediably evil. Marcuse is thus in part assimilated as a "trip" or "mind-blowing" experience in that his theory throws people deeper into their subjective reality, sharpening the discontinuity between it and the conventional reality, and ensuring that behavior will be dictated more and more exclusively by subjectivity. By comparison with this, dealing with specific questions is of secondary importance and may even prove threatening insofar as people are forced to resume contact with the universe of discourse, categories, and frames of reference of the conventional reality. ("We've got to be more realistic!") The following incident illustrates some of the principles involved.

In early June 1968, a newly graduated Syracuse University student wandered into the "Peace Office" (near the university) to get some information on the draft. He was politically liberal (vaguely opposed to the war in Vietnam but not concerned very much about anything else) and culturally straight (casual-collegiate clothes; haircut within the previous two months). The people in the office began to proselytize and finally brought him to an attic inhabited by three New Leftists for more extended argumentation. When I arrived, incense was burning profusely, acid-rock was blaring from the phonograph, and impassioned noises were being made by three or four people at once about the "evil system." The liberal could understand none of this, and tried to play the game of "getting down to specifics": "Why don't you tell me *one thing* about the system that's evil?" The answer: "Why don't *you* tell *me* one thing about the system that isn't evil!" The absence of communication was nearly total.

There are a few paragraphs at the end of *One-Dimensional Man* that appear at first glance to be tacked on in a contrived effort to give the book an upbeat ending. But these paragraphs could possibly be also seen as the germ of an understanding of the new social movements. The ideas are undeveloped and it is possible to explain the failure to develop them in terms of an individual communicant with the Marxist-humanist tradition (and therefore committed to maintaining the conscious link between reason, associated with a comprehensive historical-materialist theory of society, and revolution) confusing a *subjectivist* movement with an *irrationalist* one (such as totalitarian fascism). To clarify this, a subjectivist vanguard stands as proxy for the people: where the rationalist vanguard of a Marxist party maintains that "we *know* what the proletariat would know if only they *knew* enough," and the irrationalist vanguard of a fascist party holds that "we *will* what the people would *will* if only they were strong enough," a subjectivist vanguard claims that "we *feel* what the people would *feel* if they were allowed (or allowed themselves) to feel enough."

Marcuse correctly identifies the black and other minority lower classes as sources of new kinds of dissidence (though this is unthinkable to more traditional Marxists, who either discount such groups as a revolutionary force or even fear them as "lumpen-proletarian scum"; they cannot be *organized* and are supposedly the inevitable tool of reaction against the organized class-conscious proletariat):

> However, underneath the conservative popular base is the substratum of the outcasts and the outsiders, the exploited and persecuted of other races and colors, the unemployed and the unemployable.[6]

Marcuse at least partially understands that the new varieties of opposition are possible because the lower classes lack jobs within the large-scale organizations that are the main structural components of the system: "They exist outside the democratic process." But to say that ". . . their life is the most immediate and the most real need for ending intolerable conditions and institutions" is not to say very much, since this confuses sheer exploitation and deprivation with what is much more important here, namely, that the conventional reality is imposed as a guide to behavior only in attenuated form, thereby leaving an opening for "unrealistic," unpredictable, and orgiastic behavior which seeks to impose the reality derived from subjective experience upon the environment.

Marcuse's next sentences are somewhat more meaningful, even though he obviously perceives the black lower class in the guise in which it was polished and packaged by the black middle class for presentation to the white middle class:

> Thus their opposition is revolutionary even if their consciousness is not. Their opposition hits the system from without and is there-

> fore not deflected by the system; it is an elementary force which violates the rules of the game and, in doing so, reveals it as a rigged game. When they get together and go out into the streets, without arms, without protection, in order to ask for the most primitive civil rights, they know that they face dogs, stones, and bombs, jail, concentration camps, even death. Their force is behind every political demonstration for the victims of law and order. The fact that they start refusing to play the game may be the fact which marks the beginning of the end of a period.[7]

Marcuse's inclination to see the black lower class strictly as pathetic victims, "breaking the rules of the game"—a nebulous concept at best—seems to refer here primarily to ritually dramatized illegalities which, by calling forth acts of violent suppression on the part of the authorities, have a demystifying function; they explode delusory features of the conventional reality derived from administrative ideologies as to the well-nigh perfect "functioning" of the system. Marcuse (in 1964) obviously lacked the benefit of the historical hindsight which can now be derived from the great mass freak-outs (explosive eruptions of subjectivist consciousness onto the immediate environment) in the ghettos during July-August 1967, and April 4–11, 1968; he also wrote before the major developments in self-conscious strangeness in middle-class youth dissidence.

In New Left activist jargon (in particular among SDS activists, who consider the assimilation of *One-Dimensional Man* to be *de rigueur*), "breaking the rules of the game" has become a subjectivist concept. It has deep and powerful emotional meanings in the subculture. It now refers, in addition to, or in place of the above definition, to orgiastically joyous combat with the pigs (police); to the elimination of internalized inhibitions and restrictions on behavior through the intensification of subjectivity and the triumph of the latter over commitments to the conventional reality; and to the state of disorientation into which the contented sections of the population are thrown after having been confronted with incomprehensible weirdness, such that their adherence to the conventional reality has become attenuated, with the possibility that they might lose control or freak out themselves. This complex of meanings is illustrated by a description of the Berkeley Free Streets riot:

Sunday night (June 30th) there was a man playing a guitar walking up University Avenue. He was singing "The Times, They Are A-Changing." Behind him there was a throng of several hundred people. By the time they turned the corner nearly every window on the block was broken.

In twenty-four hours, other people were petitioning the City Council for a permit to have a mass meeting on Telegraph Avenue July 4th.

People have fought hard in the streets. All the rules of previous demonstrations have been broken. The cops used gas on a massive scale. We retaliated, for the first time, by stoning windows. They deployed goon squads in unmarked cars. We set barricades on fire, and someone even had the balls to set a cop on fire. They proclaimed a curfew and established martial law in Berkeley.

When we broke the rules of the demonstration game, we were asserting our right to control our own community. We were challenging the Establishment's definition of "law and order." We were taking what we know is ours.

The demand for freedom of assembly was tacked on afterward. Our struggle in the streets had nothing to do with petitioning our "city fathers" for permission to meet on our own turf.[8]

There is a possibility that Marcuse may have foreshadowed the Pop Front (revolutionary coalition of Soul and acid-rock) by saying:

. . . the chance is that, in this period, the historical extremes may meet again: the most advanced consciousness of humanity, and its most exploited force. It is nothing but a chance.[9]

Perhaps, on the other hand, by "the most advanced consciousness of humanity" Marcuse was actually referring (conceivably without being aware of it) to himself and a few of his old friends. After all, great philosophers committed to the principle of the sacred union of reason and revolution (with reason being understood as relating to what is purported to be a comprehensive description and negation of *objective* social reality) cannot afford to let an "elementary force" run around on the loose without giving it some fatherly guidance. However, the actual consciousness which now makes the historical encounter may not always be *advanced,* though it is interestingly *altered,* and it does supply the "concepts which bridge the gap between the present" and the future of the critical theory. This new type of consciousness does not accept the proposition (fundamental to any comprehensive historical-materialist theory of society) that objective social reality is actually *knowable* under the existing social order. That is, it is not knowable until the last confidential files are Xeroxed, the last spies are identified, and, in the words of the French student slogan, "the last sociologist is strangled in the guts of the last bureaucrat."

CHAPTER 6

Rumblings in the Gap

In the youth of the white middle class, especially among those born since World War II, there is no *experience* of anything but affluence. It is this experience, the reality of everyday life, which creates the reality gap. Not yet established in continuing adult roles and positions in the world of large-scale organizations, the Scarcity Principle, and all the apparatus of institutional and intra-psychic repressions which it supports are, quite simply, meaningless and irrelevant to them. The Depression—the last great period of sustained and *objective* scarcity—happened long before they were born. The determining effects of objective scarcity on the consciousness of a child (as perhaps communicated indirectly by other members of the family) born into the middle class during the latter years of the Depression, when part of the middle class was still dangling over the precipice of the relief rolls, and the determining effects of steadily rising affluence on the child born after World War II may be so divergent that one might almost speak of them as being on opposite sides of a cultural divide.

As we look at America, we see cities enveloped in smoke and flame. We hear sirens in the night. We see Americans dying on distant battlefields abroad. We see Americans hating each other; killing each other at home.

And as we see and hear these things, millions of Americans cry out in anguish: did we come all this way for this?

—Richard M. Nixon
(from his acceptance speech to the
1968 Republican National Convention)

If contemporary parents discover a son or daughter smoking pot in the living room, or find them arrested for incomprehensible political crimes, and then with anguished shock warn the offspring that, "You're throwing your life away. You have no idea how hard it was for us to get a college education. We *knew* what to do with our lives then! And here you are, treating the whole thing as if it's nothing!"—it will be no use. One might as well fantasize parents in the incipient stages of the agricultural revolution trying to regain control over the scandalous behavior of the young by telling them how tough things were for the tribe when everybody was scrabbling for subsistence on the hunt. Even the material possessions which have been so proudly accumulated by the parents will appear to the youth as routine, unimpressive, and already assimilated features of the environment (when they do not actually appear as repulsive instruments of repression and cultural degradation).

On one side of the reality gap, affluence is the reward of a painful struggle; on the other side, products of consumption are simply *there.* The theologian Harvey Cox is mildly amazed when, on a slumming expedition, he meets

> a lovely girl living in Haight who, when I asked her if she was worried about eating, looked at me with consummate serenity and replied, "But food *is.*"
> The hippies represent the first generation of Americans who really don't have to work for a living. No wonder they annoy us. They have dropped the bottom out of the so-called Protestant ethic.[1]

The hippies are (or perhaps *were*) in reality *assertively aware* of not having to work for a living. Having accepted affluence as a routine fact of existence, their subcultural reality demanded contempt from those who accepted institutional, cultural, and intrapsychic repression, as well as the delusory features of the conventional reality, all of this being consolidated into a structural-cultural whole by the false assumption of the scarcity of things-in-general. This contempt is perhaps epitomized by the hippies' aggressive *panhandling,* marked by accosting passers-by with the ritual question, "Got any spare change?" Here were youth, usually from middle-class or (occasionally) even wealthy families, defiantly flaunting an activity which automatically excludes one from social existence.

As for the "so-called Protestant ethic," the bottom, as I have already said, has long since been dropped out of *that* by the mass culture (a not-insignificant feature of which is the magazine to which Cox contributed the above quotation). What survives is the hallucinatory simulation of the Protestant ethic, in which the norm of compulsive effort required to satisfy contrived new needs is taken for the original and is publicly praised in conventional rhetoric as such.

During the 1960s the music that middle-class youth listened to asserted the proposition that the conventional reality is so delusory that it is at best an encumbrance. At the same time it was endlessly repeated that practically no substitute for the conventional reality, derived from being thrown deeper into the subjective experience of everyday life, or from induced intensification of experience, could possibly be more falsified. Possibly the best-known expression of this message, and qualitatively perhaps the best, is Bob Dylan's "Ballad of a Thin Man," [2] the refrain of which— ". . . something is happening here / But you don't know what it is / Do you, Mister Jones?"—is often quoted by journalists confronted by the bewildering spectacle of youthful weirdness. (A recent instance occurs in Sanche de Gramont's report on the French student revolt, "A Bas—Everything!") [3]

Mr. Jones is the personification of the conventional reality, liberal-intellectual version. He could easily be a sociologist of deviance. Sustained in the conventional reality by what appear to him as the legitimate demands of occupation and career, he internalizes these demands and repressively maintains within himself the rigid compartmentalization of feeling and intellect—starving the former while limiting, inhibiting, and sterilizing the latter. He regards cultural dissidents (and people in general) as objects of study and therefore resists experiencing them as whole and sensual beings. At the same time, his intellectual curiosity masks an anxious and fearful sense of inadequacy which has drawn him to the strange and unknown. (At several points in the song, fragments of a well-known funeral march are heard on the piano or organ; Mr. Jones has the stench of death about him.) But while he makes an effort to ingratiate himself into this alien environment, anything he might learn is negated by the fact that he will return to an environment in which the conventional reality is intact (as the sociologist of deviance withdraws from the "field"); he succumbs to the temptation to refer, within the universe of discourse of that reality, to what he has encountered as "throwing their lives away," or "data."

Mr. Jones seeks out what he understands as exciting but nevertheless despicable specimens of human deformity, in order to reinforce his sense of superiority and glamorous self-image. But he is assaulted by the universe of discourse of the alien reality, in which it is understood that the true excitement is to be derived from his own inner liberation—in which course he would be thrown so deeply into his own subjectivity that his present conceptual categories would dissolve, his points of social reference would fade, and he would no longer be able to "function" in the "real" world. For a moment he is pulled in opposite directions by discontinuous realities, but resists the temptation to leap into the unknown.

He is titillated by rebellion and at bottom treats it as an article of mass consumption or packaged entertainment. He thereby fantasizes that it is under his control, but the discontinuous reality in which it operates is thrown at him in the form of an accusation that his own reality is hallucinatory and his own way of life is incomprehensibly alien, degraded, and inferior. Meanwhile, the rebellion takes off in unpredictable ("unrealistic") directions of its own choosing, demonstrating the falsity of his assumption of omnipotence. Trying to present an image of "relevance" to fellow intellectuals, or perhaps resembling the white social scientist who enters the black ghetto armed with a battery-powered tape recorder to get supposed inside dope from people he believes to be in the know about explosive social tensions, Mr. Jones is personally excluded from the leading edge of dissidence by virtue of his inability to share the subcultural reality of the rebels; he is despised if he tries to tell them to their faces that he espouses their cause. At the same time he shares the universe of discourse of those who hallucinate the dissidence as a social pathology.

The cultural categories and concepts provided by the conventional reality seemingly become hopelessly scrambled; the environment is disorientingly inexplicable and incomprehensible; traditional sex roles become fluid, exposing and threatening those who derived satisfaction from the role rather than from sex. The cultural environment turns into a circus freak show in which it becomes unclear just who is the spectator and who is on display. Mr. Jones, disoriented by the refusal of those who dwell in rival realities to take his own conventional reality seriously, can no longer be certain as to what these alien beings are objectively capable of doing to him and his "real world" (especially in light of the anxieties and secret envy which may have driven him to approach them in the first place).

When, in the course of obtruding himself upon dissidents, he tries to advise them in terms of the political logic of the conventional reality, he is told that his role is strictly confined to being exploited and humiliated; otherwise he is superfluous. In the end he deserves only contempt and disgust; he should be made to be consistent by being deprived of all avenues of direct experience.

Dylan may be an original genius, but he hardly represents an isolated vision; this song is included in an album of which hundreds of thousands of copies have been sold since its release in 1965.

Rock lyrics provide innumerable instances of the advocacy of sex, love, hallucinogenic drugs, introspection, meditation, and the thrills of surfboard- and motorcycle-riding, as means of transcending the falsified consciousness imposed by an evil or futile society for purposes alien to what is truly human. Rock, insofar as it is created by people of about the same age as those who listen to it, is a social ideology bearing the central message that practically anything one really enjoys doing is a surer guide to where it's at (the Ultimate Truth; appropriate cultural response to objective environmental conditions; the Wave of the Future; perfection) than anything in the existing institutions of society or the received culture. In its most primitive form, as spelled out in 1964 or 1965, by The Dave Clark Five (a British group) in a song of sexual invitation called "Let Me Show You Where It's At," the message reads: "Come on, let me show you where it's at/Come on, let me show you where it's at/The name of the place is/I like it like that."

A number of songs from the Jefferson Airplane's late-1966 album *Surrealistic Pillow* illustrates the message as proclaimed just before the high tide of hippieism. "Somebody to Love" has such stirring rhythms that it sounds almost like a hippie battle hymn.

In "D.C.B.A.-25" it is mourned that, "Too many days are left unstoned," because, "I see the people of the world—what they are and what they could be." [4] The most popular of the songs in this album, "White Rabbit," is *not,* as a disc jockey on a "Top 40" radio station in Syracuse, New York, put it (perhaps in an effort to deceive parents who might have been listening), "a nice little song about Alice in Wonderland." It represents marijuana, mescaline, and so on, as alternatives to petty irrelevant, idiotic authorities and a false culture.

Jim Morrison was the leader, vocalist, and songwriter of The Doors, a group that came to prominence about a year later. His music, coupled with his long-haired, scruffy intensity and his gyrations during live performances, made him an idol of thousands of teen-age girls. *The Doors,* his group's first album, opens with "Break On Through (To The Other Side)," which proclaims that the compulsions and anxieties derived from internalization of the conventional reality may be by-passed with the derivation of a new reality from the total submergence of the self in orgasm.

Other messianic efforts to encourage and consolidate discontinuous private realities (and therefore, inevitably, a discontinuous shared subcultural reality) include a very popular song of mid-1967, "Incense and Peppermints," the title song of the first album by the Strawberry Alarm Clock. The lyrics declare that all distinctions and concepts in the universe of discourse of the conventional reality are meaningless and debilitating; that roles and social categories recognized within the conventional reality are superficial "games"; that the conventional reality is but "one point of view" and crazy as well; and that the whole thing should be rejected as a matter of self-evident necessity for purposes of self-definition.

The album by Pearls Before Swine, *One Nation Underground,* includes the song "Drop Out!" which could not possibly be more explicit in terms of the rejection of the conventional reality as coercively imposed by an evil social order.

Still more recently (1968), Ian Bruce-Douglas, the leader and songwriter of Ultimate Spinach of Boston, has written "Fragmentary March of Green," the lyrics of which are a subjectivist-ideological condemnation of the middle-class way of life; the conclusion arrived at (both logically and at the end of the song) is one which should by now be familiar to the reader: middle-class culture is so sick and deluded that in order to achieve a consciousness that represents a better apprehension of objective reality the middle-class individual must, in terms of his present frame of reference, "go insane," that is, lose his grip on the conventional reality.

Several objections could conceivably be raised at this point. First, it might be said that I have read too much into these lyrics. I also freely admit that the selections are arbitrary; but there is practically no end of other possible examples, and new releases are seemingly becoming progressively more explicit and radical in stating or even *assuming*—the existence of a shared, discontinuous reality.

Second, and more serious, it can be objected that rock is itself an integral part of the mass culture. After all, rock groups are known to do singing commercials and subject themselves to commercial exploitation even while seemingly repudiating commercialism. Big Brother and the Holding Company now record for Columbia, a *real* Big Brother and holding company. The rock record is itself obviously a product of mass consumption. And when The Mamas and the Papas sing, "You gotta go where you wanna go . . ." it seems to sound less like a call to liberation than part of the mass cultural environment, also including the current American Oil Company jingle: "You can go where you want to go . . ."

It must therefore be suspected that rock and other youth-culture manifestations function simultaneously on two different levels—or rather in two different realities. On the one hand, youth-culture elements are products of mass consumption, and are more or less accepted by everyone as such. In fact it is absolutely amazing how quickly the vocabulary and other superficial features of even the most dissident youth cultures become absorbed into the hucksterism of the mass culture. "Plymouth is tripping out this year"; "Chevrolet is happening"; Dodge offers a "groovy ride"; while Ford offers a sort of mystical illumination: "You're feeling uptight / Then you see the Light / Those better ideas from Ford / See the Light / See the Light / See the Light." *Woman's Day* magazine, which is sold at check-out counters of the A&P supermarket chain, advertised over the radio, in August 1968, that it can assist the housewife in the techniques of "psychedelic lighting for your backyard." Simultaneously, however, the youth culture represents an underground movement, necessarily created by the contradictions inherent in the reality of contemporary society, whose ultimate aim is the total destruction of this society.

The reality of daily life in the organizational middle class is, as I have indicated, elaborately linked to the conventional reality through: material comforts and advantages; demands for "realistic" behavior deriving from employment in or funding by large-scale bureaucratic organizations (corporations, state, school system or university, hospital, church); joining or "participating in" mass-membership "voluntary" organizations and "informal," "purely social," "charitable," or "civic-minded" groups, clubs, cliques, bodies, associations, and hobbyist aggregations, "belonging to" which is deemed appropriate in terms of class and status position (leading to situations which, at their most repressive, become "It's the Thing To Do if you want to get anywhere. . . . If you know what I mean."); the mass media; the hallucinatory experience of egalitarianism ("Your father/grandfather came to this country without a nickel to his name.") which subtly coalesces and inter-twines with the organizational experience of objective hierarchical authoritarianism and inequality; status and rejection anxieties of all kinds ("Oh, Mother! He didn't even *kiss* me!" "Maybe it's your mouthwash/underarm deodorant."); and the fundamental assumption of the Scarcity Principle coupled with the inevitable assumption of the availability of a sufficiency of the means of vio-lence—and the inclination to use them—to preserve some sort of distribution of things and power based on the Scarcity Principle ("law and order").

The conventional reality is thus bound to the middle-class reality-of-daily-life through an increasingly complex system of environments in which the individual "functions" as part of his established routine. Most of these environments are somehow shaped by advanced technology and many of them involve contact with persons playing highly specialized roles which, even if the complementary roles demanded of the individual are much less specialized, still impose an awareness of degrees and kinds of competence beyond his or her own possibility of mastering.

It is important to understand that *each and every change from one of these environments to another involves some alteration or adjustment of consciousness*. Some of these changes may involve severe discontinuities, as for men, when they hurriedly perform the ritual of getting up and ready for work, then drive to the city on the traffic-jammed freeway, then reorient themselves to the work situation; or for women, whose frantic activities in getting everybody off to work or school are so often followed by empty idiocy until the family dribbles back home, this being in turn followed by the time of day (late afternoon to early evening) when everybody decompresses, involving each other in a radically different kind of idiocy (or several different kinds of idiocies simultaneously).

The alternations of consciousness demanded of the individual are complicated, and shaped by the new hardware by which the individual is surrounded, either directly or indirectly (computers, solid-state home stereo phonographs and tape recorders, color television, FM radio in the car, Muzak and Xerox in the office, and perhaps, soon, home videotape recorders). Each of these media involves the use of increasingly sophisticated technology, and as Marshall McLuhan points out, each one of the media is an extension of some human physical or mental faculty: the book is an extension of the eye; clothing is an extension of the skin; the wheel is an extension of the foot; and the various electrical media are extensions of the central nervous system.

Moreover, the introduction of each new medium alters the "sense ratios" in the culture; that is, the importance of the faculty of which the medium is an extension becomes upgraded as a modality of experience relative to other faculties. For example, the spread of printing by movable type in the fifteenth century and after brought with it the predominance of the eye in the newly mass-literate cultures of Europe (mostly at the expense of the ear), and with it a new aesthetics based on the straight line and on what we call "perspective." The introduction of the book, in this view, stimulated the impulse to standardization of culture and organized social institutions, as well as the urge to categorize knowledge into neat and orderly compartments. This evolved into a cultural approach that vastly facilitated the development of technology, and developed ultimately into the culture-complex which dominated nineteenth-century industrialization: sequential processes in machine production, authoritarian bureaucracies with minutely categorized hierarchies of specialties on the military model, the neat-clean-orderly habits and living by the clock of bourgeois culture, the grid patterns in city planning.

The electric media render this culture complex obsolete by inundating the collective and individual consciousness with information enormously speeded up in flow and vastly multiplied in volume. According to McLuhan, this informational flood results in a "cultural implosion" wherein the tendencies toward "explosion," or extremely subdivided categorization and specialization, are reversed in the direction of "organic" wholeness and integrative unification of disparate elements. Specialized forms of consciousness are collapsed into a more complex version of the consciousness-structure of the primitive tribal community, specialized organizations are collapsed into systems, and the distinction between public and private consciousness disappears.

McLuhan believes that the distinction between public and private consciousness was rigidified by print technology, since the latter encourages the emergence of the "private point of view" of the author, and also because the book or printed matter is read by the single reader "in private." This notion should be put in proper perspective and understood as a facilitation of the development of bourgeois society, as Polanyi understood it. Just as the bourgeoisie very briefly secured the predominance of the self-regulating market over society, it also established a "free market of ideas" as well as the bourgeois intellectual freedoms based on the principles of the sanctity of intellectual choices made by producers and consumers of culture and the inviolability of individual intellectual property. This obviously did not prevent considerable standarization of consciousness (a sort of intellectual proletarianization) among the mass of the literate population.

McLuhan believes that intellectual processes based on sorting and categorizing will be replaced by processes based on "pattern recognition." This is another way of saying that higher-order intellectual processes and the conceptual ordering of perceptions of social reality will inevitably become subjectivistic, or at least colored by subjectivity. McLuhan's references to "pattern recognition" draw analogies with the information-processing operations of computers. But no human being recognizes a pattern without his total emotional life coming into play; I recall one scholar's reference to his "breakthrough into virgin territory."

The new media, therefore, by their specific properties (in addition to the mass-culture content already discussed) put pressure on the compartmentalization of subjectivity and "public" life enforced within the organizational subcultures to which the middle classes are committed. But there is worse. Each one of the media is a distinctive mode of recording, reproducing, and representing the "real" world requiring a specific adjustment of consciousness and a specific mode of inner-subjective involvement with it. A film seen in a theater is not *quite* the same thing when seen on television. The individual gets inklings of the degree to which "reality" can be falsified or distorted by means of the technical versatility of the new media, without any deliberately manipulative intent such as that of which we speak when we refer to "managed news" and "pseudoevents." It is possible to experiment in one's own living room with manipulating the tone and balance control of the stereo set; splicing, mixing, and editing tapes; and playing tricks on the home-movie camera.

The reaction to the war in Vietnam provides an illustration of the role of the new media in widening reality gaps. The war has met with overt opposition within the middle classes in a manner and degree that the Korean War never did. A partial cause of this is seen by journalists and others in the so-called "credibility gap," defined as conspicuous and self-evident lying by high dignitaries of state, including the President. But "credibility gaps" do not arise merely because the government is lying. Every "realistic" citizen knows that the government lies; it does so in the "national interest." But given the nightly juxtapositions, on the television evening news, of the official lies with the on-the-spot coverage of the war, the conventional logic which the government expects of the viewer is made conscious, and therefore increasingly repellent: "The government never lies. But the government lies in fighting communism, and therefore is preserving freedom. When the government lies, this is to be carefully distinguished from the lies of the 'enemy's' communist propaganda which is understood to be false because of the communistic nature of their system." With the expansion of the war, this conventional logic became more and more obviously backed by the use of force and the formulation of an even more twisted logic on the right of dissent: "This war is being fought to protect your right of dissent. Therefore, if you want to preserve your civil liberties you will keep your mouth shut. And if you don't like it, weirdo, you can go to China."

Millions of people still follow these and other aspects of the logic required to sustain the hallucinations with which the war is rationalized. This might be a triumph of the conventional reality comparable to what is involved in simultaneously producing thermonuclear weapons and financing the purchase of suburban houses on thirty-year mortgages. Those who take an unmitigatedly hallucinatory view of the war, as well as millions more whose hallucinations are mitigated by "realistic considerations of national interest" (i.e., the war is lost or "militarily unwinnable"), are people whose will to believe is sustained by the fact that no other logic is *possible* for them given the assumptions of the conventional reality in which they live and which proceeds from the social structure in a manner already described. But just as the United States Army was called upon to safeguard a rigged election in South Vietnam in 1967, it was called upon in 1968 to safeguard a rigged Democratic National Convention in Chicago. Perhaps, in the scheme of official values of the time, it was to be counted a "moral victory" that the convention "could be held at all."

But it is not only in such dramatic developments that the difficulties in maintaining hold on the conventional reality are observed. It is clear that immense numbers of people in this society, especially in the middle classes, cannot or at least do not perform the complex adjustments of consciousness demanded by the routines of daily life without considerable chemical assistance. When the President of the United States, in his 1968 State of the Union Message, proclaims a holy crusade against those who tempt youth into the "slavery" of LSD and marijuana, it is conveniently forgotten that:

> America is the most drug-ridden society in history. The average "straight" American adult consumes from three to five mind-altering drugs a day. . . . From infancy onward, children are directly and indirectly taught by parents, television, movies and advertising that every time they have a pain or a problem, they should "solve" it by taking something. The alcohol, tobacco and pill industries spend hundreds of millions of dollars annually to

encourage and promote maximum use of their products, each associating its drug with youthfulness and happiness.[5]

A glance through the "slick" weekly magazine, *Medical World News,* which seems to exist for the sole purpose of carrying advertisements for drugs, many of them the tranquilizer and antidepressant type, leads one to speculate, in fact, about who is making addicts out of whom. To give just a few brief examples: from the April 23, 1965, issue (page 62)—picture: faded photograph of plump young woman in bathing costume of late nineteenth century; the caption reads:

> Adorable then . . . deplorable now. In overweight . . . control food and mood all day long with a single morning dose. AMBAR No. 1 EXTENTABS/AMBAR No. 2 EXTENTABS (A. H. Robins Co.) [6]

This substance contains methedrine and phenobarbital, two addictive drugs. The physician is being propagandized to believe that conformity to mass-culture standards of feminine attractiveness is a worthy use of drugs whose possession by teen-agers without prescription "for kicks" is severely punished. Meanwhile, in an advertisement for an amphetamine mixed with a tranquilizer on page 71 of the same issue: picture—drawing in brown and white of balding executive in shirt sleeves and wearing necktie, seated at desk and gesturing force fully with right hand which holds a pencil. Caption reads:

> Regained: the ability to make decisions, the emotional energy to complete his work. DEXAMYL helps relieve symptoms of mild depression within the hour. (Smith Kline & French Labs.) [7]

Or from the October 14, 1966, issue (pp. 68–69)—picture: full-page black-and-white photograph of young mother clutching her head as she gives her little girl a bath. Partial text,

> HER KIND OF PRESSURES LAST ALL DAY . . . shouldn't her tranquilizer? Meprospan/400 sustained-released tranquilizer for sustained anxiety and tension. Daytime dose helps keep patient calm throughout the day. Nighttime dose fosters restful sleep throughout the night.[8]

What is relevant here about the sedatives, stimulants, and tranquilizers is that they minimize or suppress subjectivity. The sedatives calm one down when some inconvenient emotion threat-

ens to disrupt one's established pattern of interpersonal relationships, or even put one to sleep if there is some emotionally
troublesome thought keeping one awake. The tranquilizers help one
to "get through the day" by maintaining one's calm in office or
household situations where friction or tension would otherwise
disrupt "useful" and "productive" activity. The central-nervous-
system stimulants, such as the drugs of the amphetamine family,
keep one compulsively preoccupied with some "productive" activity, reducing the tendency to ruminate and "waste time"; they also
reduce the sex and hunger drives. Alcohol, while lowering certain
inhibitions, tends to fog and dull the senses, while blurring over
some of the more complex (and therefore threatening, because
ambivalent, anxious, and depressing) subjective states. It is not
surprising that "straights" see nothing peculiar in their own drug
dependencies, since the chemicals help them to "function" and to
perform culturally commendable activities; meanwhile the "hallucinogenic" drugs are consumed by people who not only enjoy
them conspicuously, but also show no intention of "functioning"
or being useful to anybody in authority.

If, as conventional critics claim, hippies and teen-agers take
drugs to "escape reality," the implications of this widespread and
legitimatized adult middle-class form of escape—the product of
eager collaboration between the drug companies, the medical profession, and the patients themselves—are horrifying indeed.

Daily life within the middle classes is not on the whole scarred
by violence, authoritarian brutality, or strenuous physical exertion;
by comparison with what most people have to go through in this
world, that way of life is a pretty soft touch. The middle classes are
in no position to pity themselves or to demand pity from others.
Yet when certain people complain of "the stresses and strains of
modern living," they refer to real irrational repressions in terms of
authoritarian structures and intrapsychic mechanism; these are employed to maintain conventional reality on the collective and
individual levels, despite the growing pressure on the compartmentalization of subjectivity and "public" life and the complex
alterations of consciousness required as new kinds of environments
are invented. A stereotyped situation is presented in a patent-
medicine commercial which begins with the loud blare of an

idiotic and incomprehensible rock song. A housewife screams, *"Turn that thing down"* and then moans, "Oh, my *head!"* A soothing voice persuades her to try a substance called Cope: "That's spelled C-O-P-E. . . . Unlike *ordinary* headache remedies, which only cure the pain of ordinary headaches, Cope is specially designed for today's *nervous tension* headaches." Presumably, the market researchers concluded that large numbers of middle-class people cannot cope. A housewife hearing this commercial over WHEN in Syracuse can be forgiven for not realizing that her teen-age offspring, who listen to the Top-40 station WNDR are being propagandized to use altogether different chemical counteragents for nervous tension (as well as other forms of tension-avoidance procedures). The teen-ager can be forgiven for perceiving the irrationality in the fact that his drugs are illegal and stigmatized, while Mother's are not.

The pressure increases, and the hallucinations grow more pronounced and exaggerated so long as the Scarcity Principle continues to be assumed. But the absence of the Scarcity Principle implies total social revolution and restructuring of all organized institutions. It sometimes appears that the middle-class individual who dwells within the conventional reality seems to be clutching himself to keep from slipping away; expressions like "get a hold on yourself" and "get a grip on yourself" abound in popular speech. It is somewhat disturbing when the Sheraton hotel chain advertises its establishments in various cities with a picture of an executive in a business suit, wearing a hat, and carrying an attaché case, but looking like a mechanical doll with a huge windup key in his back. ("Going to Chicago? Keyed-up executives unwind at the Sheraton-Chicago Hotel.") The freak, having grown up in a middle class in which the threat of actual scarcity had disappeared, calls the conventional middle-class individual, despite the latter's appearance of glad-handing informality, "up-tight straight"; calls his personality "plastic" (an attractively packaged product of mass consumption); and dismisses his elaborately calculated and carefully distinguished set of roles as "games."

Perhaps encouraged by fascination with hippieism, many people in the middle classes have become aware of their psychic disabilities, though not necessarily of the institutions which generate and sustain them. Thus, since 1967–1968, "sensitivity

training," "the psychology of being," and the Transcendental
Meditation cult of the Maharishi Mahesh Yogi have become
widespread middle-class fads. These practices all include the development of subjectivity so as to achieve "inner joy" and
deeper communication with one's fellowman. They assist the
individual to have a more tolerable inner life, while, generally
speaking, either ignoring or accepting the formal structure of the
external environment. One achieves "communication" or "dialogue" with authorities, rather than attacking them. The Maharishi,
in particular, urges accommodation to all authority figures, whether
parent or political leaders; he upholds obedience to the law.

"Sensitivity training" and the like can be assimilated within
the middle class as a new sort of tranquilizer; it makes things easier
at the office and makes anxiety-inducing developments easier to
put up with. Or else it can degenerate into the faddish manifestations of intellectual in-groups. Still another possibility is that the
enhanced subjectivity will be assimilated as a compartmentalized
faculty to be used where it is "realistic" and expedient to do so.

The freak stereotype of "straightness": "Whiteman," by Robert Crumb (from *R. Crumb's Head Comix*, Viking Press, New York, 1968).

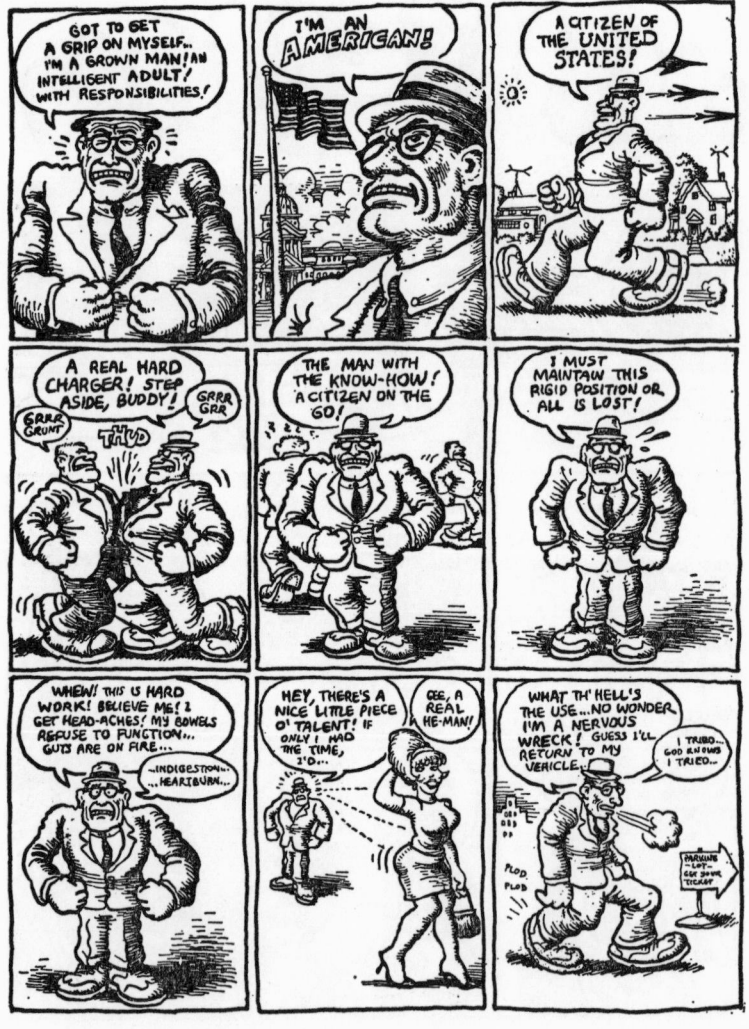

PART III

THE POLITICS OF TOTAL
CULTURAL EXPERIENCE

"wanted
roomate

.　.　.

to live (co-operatively)

with
psychedelic
　　marxists

.　.　.

call 479-6532
　cheap

.　.　.

　　(handwritten advertisement posted on window
　　of the Gridiron Restaurant, two blocks from
　　Syracuse University, June 1968.)

"Je suis marxiste, tendance groucho."
　　(French student slogan, Paris, May 1968.)

CHAPTER 7

Introducing the Freak

The dissident youth subculture, recently arisen, rejects the middle-class mass culture and the purposes of repressive consumption that it serves. At the same time, the subculture reflects the impact of the same mass culture as a major environmental feature of the society.

The new youth cultures are, most conspicuously, even more subjectivist and situationally minded than the mass culture itself; this is true of youth in both the black lower class and the white middle class (in the discussion following, I will be describing the latter, mostly). In both groups there is contempt for the absurdities of repressive consumption. In both there is a rejection of the mass culture for linking subjective gratifications to the ownership of material objects; for its superficiality, denial of "real" emotional gratification, and inhibition of self-discovery; and, most importantly, for its being ignorant, or denying the reality, of its *own* subjective experience. Both groups have been accustomed to television in the home almost since their birth. (Television is an absolute necessity of life in even the most abysmally poor households in the urban black ghetto. It is a vehicle for escapism and is almost indispensable for pacifying the children. In many homes, the set

is almost never shut off.) Both groups have been bombarded for
years with appeals to subjectivity and immediacy of experience.
("New Ultra-Bright toothpaste / For a taste you can really
FEEL / New Ultra-Bright gives your mouth / SEX APPEAL.")
And perhaps most important, both groups have absorbed vast
amounts of unintentionally communicated information and re-
shaped it into new patterns.

It may disturb some Americans to discover that a number of
youths (as of 1967–1968) have been referring to themselves with
pride as "freaks," or that expressions such as "it's freaky, man" or
"that really freaked me out" are used in a positive sense. But that
is part of the whole point. While only a minority of the members
of the subcultures in which I am interested use the term "freak" as
a way of identifying themselves, it nevertheless can be used to
make a sociological point: "Freaks"—as I use the term—are
visibly members of middle-class youth subcultures which include
a subcultural reality in complete discontinuity with the conventional reality. Freaks are walking counterenvironments who, by
dwelling within their subjective realities or shared subcultural
reality, come to assert the right to total control over their physical
appearance and outward behavior—to the total irrelevance of the
culture and informal norms of those who dwell within the conventional reality (any compromise of the demands of the inner reality,
when these are known to be in contradiction with the "outside"
culture, being known as a "cop-out"), except insofar as it is desired to stimulate *disorientation* among the cultural enemy. On the
subject of disorientation, a long-haired and bearded Syracuse New
Leftist said bluntly, "When people see me coming down the street,
they just *have* to notice."

"Freak" denotes an ideal type which embraces the hippie
(1965–1967) and New Left (1967–?) subcultures. But the fact
that the word is also used for purposes of self-identification requires a little refinement of definition. American affluence is a
New Thing in history; the freak, one form of its dialectical an-
tithesis, is also a New Thing in history: a cultural mutant. Hippies
and sympathizers, during the "button craze" of 1966–1967, wore
(among hundreds of other slogans) pins with the legend, "FREAK
FREELY"; yippies (Youth International Party) in New York
City threaten the authorities with "Street Freak Germ Warfare";

the Mothers of Invention sing a defiant song of contempt for the American educational system called "Hungry Freaks, Daddy!"

The verses of the two songs contrast the usages of "freak." The first is defiantly hostile and aggressively obnoxious. The second is a gentle display of magical ethereal inner liberation. In both cases one finds a derivation of the "freak" self-identification from the enemy culture's categories, but it is also combined with an assertion of self-conscious weirdness directed at the disorientation and destruction of that culture. This is to be done in the first case through the direct expression of hostility—in historically new forms of course; in the second, through the seductive inner power of magical beauty. The difference, I suppose, lies in whether the enemy is despised or pitied, and in the value placed upon revenge as opposed to the desire for the enemy's personal redemption and reclamation.

As with so much of youth-culture jargon, the meanings attached to "freak" display all kinds of nebulous ambiguities. Just as the cultural dissident will adopt the categorization placed upon him by his "up-tight" cultural enemies and then assertively throw it back in their faces in a fashion almost exactly parallel to that in which the Black Nationalist throws soul food, emotionalism, and "natural rhythm" back in the white man's face, so he will *simultaneously* reassure himself of the validity of his own reality and the hallucinatory quality of the conventional reality, and the culture in which it is embedded, by stigmatizing participants in the enemy culture as "freaks." The tripped-out acid-head will notice conventional-looking individuals performing some conventional-looking, ritualized, routine, or standardized activity and then, having a vision of its empty, futile, dehumanized, and alienated quality, will collapse in helpless giggling, while exclaiming, "What a freak," or, "What a bunch of freaks." He might then end up with an insight into the unity of the cosmos: "Everything's so freaky—oh, wow, man, people are beautiful, it's all so groovy!" Bearing in mind, then, the influence of the inner life on semantics, it makes sense that, in the same leaflet in which they threaten the authorities with "Street Freak Germ Warfare," the yippies also, by way of venting their spleen on respectable middle-class tourists seen as polluting their environment by sight-seeing (the street freaks being the sights), refer to "Uptown Freaks."

Since in these dissident cultures compulsive behavior tends to be defined as morally evil, we find "freak" used in a pejorative sense to denote an addict or compulsive. There occur such usages as "speed-freak" (addicted to methedrine or other stimulants of the amphetamine family); "bike-freak" (motorcycle fetishist); "power-freak" (domineering authoritarian figure); "violence-freak" (someone twisted and corrupted by blood lust, or, in a usage newly become obsolete, a dissident obsessed with ideas of violent rebellion); "structure-freak" (one who emphasizes order and hierarchy at the expense of spontaneity); and "print-freak" (one who reads or writes prose to the exclusion of interest in, or creation in, media considered by McLuhan to be more appropriate to the Electric Age).

With "freak-out," also, there are dangers of confusion. For a start, I will define this term as the "explosive eruption of subjectivist consciousness onto the immediate environment." The freak-out is a sudden and essentially spontaneous event in which participants in a dissident subculture (which is in turn part of a broader social movement marked by the appearance of new forms of subjectivist consciousness) act on their environment solely in terms prescribed by the subjective reality. A freak-out may be either individual or (more dramatically) collective. During such an event, the dissidents orgiastically impose their own cultural meanings on the environment, using all the means at their disposal that the subculture considers morally valid at the time. They are at the same time effacing the cultural meanings imposed forcibly (in the routine condition of society) as manifestations of the cultural-political enemy; the result (if it lasts long enough) may be called by some such fantasy term as a "free commune" or "liberated area."

Frank Zappa, the creator, founder, guiding genius, and ideologist of The Mothers of Invention, can be credited at the very least with greatly broadening the meaning of "freak" and "freak-out," and associating it with a social movement and with the subjectivist ideological consciousness crystallizing among thousands of middle-class youths as of 1965–1966. Zappa's style, in concert, on records, and in print, emphasizes deliberate obnoxiousness. In the album-cover notes to *Freak-Out,* he describes himself thus:

Frank Zappa is the leader and musical director of THE MOTHERS OF INVENTION. His performances in person with the group are rare. His personality is so repellent that it's best he stay away . . . for the sake of impressionable young minds who might not be prepared to cope with him. When he does show up he performs on the guitar. Sometimes he sings. Sometimes he talks to the audience. Sometimes there is trouble.

Two inches above this is some writing in fine print:

"WHAT IS 'FREAKING OUT' "
On a personal level, *Freaking Out* is a process whereby an individual casts off outmoded and restricting standards of thinking, dress, and social etiquette in order to express CREATIVELY his relationship to his immediate environment and the social structure as a whole. Less perceptive individuals have referred to us who have chosen this way of thinking and FEELING as *"Freaks,"* hence the term: *Freaking Out*. On a collective level, when any number of *"Freaks"* gather and express themselves creatively through music or dance, for example, it is generally referred to as a *FREAK OUT*. The participants, already emancipated from our national *social slavery,* dressed in their most inspired apparel, realize as a group whatever potential they possess for *free expression.* We would like to encourage everyone who HEARS this music to join us . . . become a member of *The United Mutations* . . . *FREAK OUT!*

A description of a freak-out from the *Washington Free Press* (December 1-15, 1968):

When you're in the aisles of the Fillmore East full of a thousand people stoned, laughing, dancing to music so intense it fills your body. When you're in the Fillmore liberated feeling the warmth of a thousand people. Splashing against the walls in more colours than a light show. Young naked men and women dancing amid flags and lights and we could turn to each other freely to dance, rap, touch, laugh because there was no fear. There was no fear in that community who could have made love or revolution at that moment, with equal ease. And in a flash of colours you know the difference between revolution as an act of love—and war as an act of hate. It would have taken an army of police to have hassled any one of that community. You return to this federal city full of polite death and feel longing in your guts for something beautiful that's dying here.
     We don't know what's going down in our immediate future, but it's inevitable that whether we are building our homes, con-

fronting the vast American monster or filling the streets with our insistence, we will have to have formed a community so strong that it will be capable of maintaining joy amidst struggle. When we lose the ability to throw open our arms in laughter at our own madness and deal with our visions amidst absurdity we are becoming the monster we are doing battle with.

If in the midst of chaos, we can remember who we are, and carefully listen to each other, we will hear beautiful things filling the air.

In advanced industrial society, with its expanded availability of transportation and cosmopolitan contacts, "communities," as patterns of informal human association associated with fixed geographical locations, become obsolete. They are replaced by "scenes": patterns of human association consolidated almost entirely by subculture and intense interaction which are associated with specific points on the map almost as a matter of historical accident (in the ideal-typical limiting case). The "black community" and the "free community" may be associated with specific neighborhoods for a period of years, but the most important activity, in terms of the consolidation of the collectivity, takes place fluidly, in the *street*. When a freak-out occurs, therefore, the people of the dissident subculture will loot, paint, infest, burn things, or otherwise leave their mark on the street or on other places of casual gathering such as public and university buildings or perhaps factories and subway stations. People "freak out" on their *own scenes:* they insist on controlling environments where they happen to be *at the time,* in utter disregard of "property rights" and other institutional arrangements. "The street belongs to the people. Liberate the street!" "We ARE the people!"

We have been conditioned by our culture to understand that political behavior in social movements—as under more static conditions—must be deliberately organized. Political behavior is therefore supposed to be understood as disciplined dissidents marching, with either ballot papers or rifles in hand, with the intention of either replacing the personnel of existing institutions or replacing the institutions themselves with substitutes prepared in advance. The freak-out ignores the political logic of industrial society. Its meaning to the participants—an orgiastic acting-out of a discontinuous, publicly submerged, and perhaps even consciously submerged subcultural reality—is the only meaning they are concerned about. I therefore relate the phenomenon of the freak-out to the social-structural conditions which bring discontinuous realities into being, the at-least-momentary disruption of conventionally organized society in the environments freaked-out upon. Thus, in Detroit, where the affluent were sucked into the freak-out of the poor:

> There apparently was, on that first day, a feeling of unwonted elation among those who ran in the streets. An articulate young black nationalist whom I met, a student at Wayne State University with a bright, fluid mind told me, poking at the nosepiece of his horn-rimmed glasses to push them into place, fingering the tuft of beard under his lip: "There was a new thing, a new feeling, out there on Twelfth Street. I was out there Sunday. It was between noon and two o'clock that the feeling changed. After all those years of having the man in control—Detroit's an affluent town, Detroit's black people are well-off—not middle class, not even lower-middle, but upper-proletariat, I mean a cat can finish high school and get a job at a factory and buy a Pontiac and ride around and all, but the man has his finger on you every minute of the day. I mean, "Show up at *this* time," and, "Do *this* on the assembly line," and every minute of the day it's been what *he's* said. And you get home, and the man is your landlord, and so on and so on. But out there, there was suddenly a realization. Man, the whole thing was *reversed*." [1]

Or in France, where the poor were sucked into the freak-out of the affluent:

> Every institution, every authority was called into question and for a moment disappeared altogether: there was no sovereign power, no more state, no more government, and there were no more political parties. On the barricades of the Rue Gay-Lussac Cohn-Bendit made a historic speech: "I call upon the working class to join our struggle!" And the working class seemed to respond to this young man whom *L'Humanité* and *Minute* (the Communists and Fascists) described as a "German Jewish agitator."
>
> On May 13—against the party that claimed to represent it, against the trade-union organization that up to now had represented it best—the working class threw itself into a 24-hour strike. But this was only a prelude to another strike—a strike such as France had never seen. Joining the students who sought "student power" in the heart of the universities, the workers refused to limit their demands solely to material betterment. Despite the CGT (Confédération Générale du Travail) which resisted as much as

possible, the workers demanded "worker power" in the factories. This is revolution! [2]

In both cases, specific economic, political, and institutional grievances become submerged beneath the billowing-up of a highly individual disgust with being treated as only a part of one's self, with that part being meshed into some idiotic routine. The freak-out explodes into a place which is also a "scene"—a locus of a subculture most meaningful to the participants in terms of their *whole beings;* and it constitutes the collective posing of the question, "WHY THE FUCK HAVE I BEEN PUTTING UP WITH ALL THIS SHIT?"

In advanced industrial society, we find revolutionary implications in the enormous headlines on the front page of the *Los Angeles Free Press* for October 6–12, 1967:

WHY DID YOU
GET UP
THIS MORNING

WHAT
ARE YOU
AFRAID OF [3]

CHAPTER 8

Inside the Freak

Since the middle-class youth does not directly experience the conditions of objective scarcity, it is possible to derive an explanation of the distinctive world view and cultural-political manifestations of the freak of middle-class origin. That is to say, the freak believes what he feels, while his cultural antagonist, the "up-tight straight" of the same age, tries to feel what he believes.

It is obvious that adherence to the conventional reality also seems to have worn quite thin in many of the more intelligent and sensitive of the "straights." Notable in this connection are the dedicated young men and women who, in 1968, campaigned for Senator Eugene McCarthy "to give the system one last chance." One of them was interviewed in the August 20, 1968 issue of *Look* (which reached the newsstands just prior to the Republican National Convention):

> Representing the best of [the McCarthy workers], 23-year-old Dianne Dumanoski of Gardner, Mass., walked away from her Ph.D. fellowship at Yale to work as a volunteer for McCarthy. A soft-voiced, wispy blonde, she recalled that her political activism began when a friend telephoned her at Yale last February and asked, "Can you leave for New Hampshire in an hour?" She

could and did. She was a coordinator of McCarthy's young volunteers there and has continued the work in other primaries and
in delegate fights.

Dianne was graduated from Vassar, an English major, in 1966.
She also dances, fences, speaks Russian and writes short stories
and poems. . . .[1]

But this paragon seems at times to talk like a plain-clothes dropout:

"I'm good at being in school, but that's not necessarily where
I should be," she said. "A lot of cloddy people are in graduate
school. You have to listen to boring things being said by boring
people who are bored with what they say and bored with themselves. Ninety-nine percent of what is written in scholarly journals
is garbage. The big "they"—they are forcing my generation to
act, and we're only just learning how. We scared the Johnson
people in New Hampshire. I must say that you get a great deal
of exultation out of scaring the old people. . . . It is very sad for
intelligent, talented people not to be able to plug in. . . . Politics
is a big machine, and we're still out of it, we can't control it." [2]

Freak consciousness shows an amazing capacity to survive or
even develop under the most inhospitable possible circumstances,
as is indicated by the steady trickle of letters from servicemen in
Vietnam to "underground" publications. This is a letter from a
Marine, written in mid-1967 (when the Marine Corps still con-
sisted almost entirely of volunteers rather than conscripts):

Dear EVO:
I am a Marine, and if that isn't bad enough, I am in Vietnam,
and that is definitely a BUMMER.

And I would just like to let you know one thing. Without grass,
EVO, and the [Los Angeles] Free Press, I wouldn't be able to
hack this place.

The squares in this place are definitely worse than [San Fran-
cisco] Chief of Police Cahill ever thought of being. No one is
safe from the prying eyes of this "free" totalitarian government
in which we live.

WE wish to thank you for giving us something to groove out
ON, live FOR, and return TO.
                              Your Fellow Dropouts (in arms)
P.S. We wish to remain anonymous, out of fear of reprisals by the
military establishment.[3]

Also impressive as an indication of the precariousness with
which the conventional reality is imposed on much of middle-class
youth is the ease and thoroughness with which individuals can be

converted, or rather "freaked out" of one reality and into another, as the result of intense experiences in sex, drug use, or political confrontation. During political confrontations, sudden transformations of consciousness or "radicalization" can involve hundreds or thousands of people, chiefly as a result of being victimized by or witnessing police atrocities (as happened frequently at Columbia University in spring, 1968, and at Chicago that summer).

J. Anthony Lukas of *The New York Times* reported the August 29 late evening rally in Grant Park, across the street from the Conrad Hilton Hotel:

> Take the case of Scott Vondran, an 18-year-old student. Late Wednesday night, Mr. Vondran told a newsman: "I was walking down Wabash Avenue when somebody yelled, 'The cops are coming!' We went into a store and the cops started pushing everyone in after us. They came in and arrested eight of us. I was never for all this peace stuff until tonight. Now I am."
>
> The militant mood of the young people in front of the Hilton yesterday was made particularly clear when former Gov. Endicott Peabody of Massachusetts, a convention delegate, mounted an upturned ashcan to speak.
>
> Mr. Peabody appealed to the youths not to let the "sickening violence" and Senator Eugene J. McCarthy's defeat the night before drive them into the streets.
>
> "Whatever you do, stay in the political process," he shouted, his hands outstretched to his young listeners, many of them neatly dressed young men and women wearing McCarthy buttons.
>
> But he met chiefly stone-faced stares and cries of "Sit down, old man!" or "Up against the wall!"
>
> Yesterday afternoon speaker after speaker talked of "going into the streets," "spilling some blood" and "setting up an American liberation front." (*New York Times,* August 31, 1968)

What accounts for this volatility of consciousness and for the widespread totalistic rhetoric about "system" and "Establishment" among so much of middle-class youth?

Obviously, if the Scarcity Principle is not operative, then the intricate cultural motivational calculus of profit and loss, success and failure, pleasure and suffering, reward and punishment, achievement and stasis, status and rejection becomes irrelevant—or, more accurately, one might say that the psychic mechanisms involved cease to be an interconnected whole. Instead, they become a collection of disjointed moving parts only tenuously related to each other and to a central inner-psychic motivational driving force.

The unconscious acceptance of the Scarcity Principle facilitates the imposition upon individual motivation of a seamless web of needs, from those which are objectively life-sustaining to those which are grotesquely contrived. If the products of consumption are, as a general principle, scarce, and all are translatable into money (cash or credit), then they are all *achieved, striven for,* and *accumulated.* Vast quantities of food are accumulated in the deep freeze and the twenty-seven-cubic-foot refrigerator—which are themselves accumulated.

The irrelevance of the Scarcity Principle, on the other hand, facilitates an "I-can-make-it" attitude where certain life-preserving necessities are taken for granted or at least regarded as "no big thing" or "nothing to get hung up about." A distinction can now arise—and become intensely clear—between these necessities and other consumer goods for which contrived needs have been implanted in the consuming public. The freak, while not an ascetic, refuses to burden himself with fixed institutional ties, fixed residence, or formalized personal relationships, insofar as these may be necessary for him to accumulate material possessions. He develops an alternative hierarchy of needs in which the paramount values are the intensification and deepening of subjective experience and emotional life, as well as the continuing creation of the self. Drugs have an obvious importance for these purposes. So, for a good number of people, does the stereo set, because of the importance of music in the creation of a total environment for in-depth involvement. One sometimes finds a "pad" in which there is no furniture at all, though an expensive set of stereo components can be seen lined up against a wall.

The vital consumer-goods sector of the economy is sustained by the creation and manipulation of artificial needs which are further removed from "human needs"—whatever they are. And just exactly what "human needs" are is in this context much less relevant than the fact that contrived need is pyramided on top of contrived need (i.e., once you have implanted in me the need for your new mint-flavored fluoridated toothpaste, which gets my mouth in the proper condition for sex, you instill in me the craving for your electric toothbrush to put the paste on, so that my mouth gets a groovy erotic massage and I am in the proper mood for making love). Meanwhile, the delayed personality and cultural consequences of the post-World War II prosperity have brought into being a generation which gets a drastically reduced psychic gain from consuming goods.

The Scarcity Principle, when thoroughly internalized, has a constricting effect on the behavior conceivable in relation to authority figures or in situations structured by them. All authority figures, obviously, control, modify, or manipulate behavior through the potential or routine use of sanctions. In the case of most authority figures outside the family (and, in the middle classes, within the family) with whom the individual routinely comes into contact, these sanctions are limited to the granting or withholding of material or symbolic rewards which have immediate effects upon the individual's physical or psychic well-being and to the placing of some kind of notation on his "record," which can have long-term and indefinite (and therefore all the more anxiety-provoking) effects on his life chances. Rewards are granted to subordinates upon the successful or adequate performance of role-behaviors with definable boundaries. Sanctions routinely used by authority figures are removed by several degrees of severity from the coercive violence upon which hierarchical authority ultimately depends. Normally, the subordinate will so thoroughly internalize the role-behaviors anticipated of him that he will not even be consciously aware of the potential recourse to violence. The limitation of conceivable behaviors in structured relationships with authority figures has the effect, in turn, of narrowing the range of conceivable behaviors in all other roles; meanwhile the predictable performance by other people of complementary roles even in "casual" and "informal" situations becomes endowed with some of the repressive impact of sanctions used by authority figures—symbolic rewards or punishments which tend to sustain the predictability of the individual's own behavior.

These elementary propositions are subject to modifications given the attenuation of the Scarcity Principle in the everyday life of the individual. The experience from earliest childhood that the means of sustenance are to be taken as a given and assumed feature of the total societal environment (outside as well as inside the family)—manna from heaven lying on the ground for the taking, if you will—makes hash of the prevailing cultural assumptions of the relationship between behaviors and rewards. This starts in the family and goes beyond "permissive child-training practices." No matter what child-training methods are favored by the parents, they are under intense pressures to consume. They will therefore *unconsciously* lavish all kinds of abundance on the children; or *consciously* seek to bestow upon them "advantages we never had"; or be *nagged* into coming across with the goodies by the children themselves from the time when they are able to make invidious comparisons with what is available to playmates, classmates, "kids on the block"; or will surround *themselves* with consumer goods such that a sense of affluence is unmistakably communicated to, and internalized by, the children. Moreover, the child growing up in a homogeneous middle-class neighborhood (or otherwise encapsulated middle-class environment), and going to a "good" school (i.e., middle class and white), comes to have not even the remotest possibility of conceiving of a nonaffluent standard of living as something into which he is seriously threatened with falling because of his own or his family's personal shortcomings, or because of the vagaries of the business cycle.

This child has grown up with television (the content of which is the way of life of the white middle class). He has probably grown up experiencing the fixation of his parents upon formal education (the content of which is the way of life of the white middle class); a college education is represented as being at least as inevitable for him as death and taxes. The availability of, at minimum, effortless sustenance has become so assumed by him and so assured to him that he understands it to be far more than merely *secure;* it is *traditional.*

The attenuation of the Scarcity Principle which is built into the "socialization" of middle-class youth, especially those born since World War II, means inevitably, therefore, that a major psychic, cohesive force which in the "modal personality" constricts role-behaviors conceivable in relationships with authority figures (and therefore in all roles to some extent) has been critically weakened. That is, the youth discovers through experience that he can do a great many more things than he was *taught* he could without suffering what are *to him* irreparable and disastrous consequences; though the same doings may appear to his parents and others in authority as "ruining his life" or "throwing his life away." Such a personality will therefore exhibit a tendency to elaborate new behavioral responses and initiatives in hierarchical situations. All kinds of innovations will casually be made in these role situations, ranging from changes that are small, subtle, and unconscious to those that are gross, obvious, and conscious, and they will often occur for no better reason than the fact that the individual in question happens to do whatever-it-is at the time; and generally feels that there is no good reason why it should not be. If the authorities in question react repressively to the new styles, vocabulary, or whatever, then the individual will experience the authorities, as well as the institution which they represent, as stifling, if not intolerable. Since the youth tend to make such demands upon all authorities within all environments and institutions with which they come into contact (family, school, large-scale organizations of all kinds), and since practically none of these institutions, including those undergoing liberalization, have the scope for accommodating themselves to the unprecedented demands for the tolerance, acceptance, or adoption of innovations which the youth are presenting, the tendency is to experience a stifling and somewhat undifferentiated coalition of repressive forces.

The authorities, who regard with pride, or even in some cases with trepidation, the amount of liberalization they are (or think they are) permitting, find that the youths to whom they try to appeal regard the recent changes as inconsequential. Middle-class youth experience a generalized restrictiveness in all the mass-cultural patterns of the parental generation, and in all the organized institutions dominated by it; authority figures appear to be afflicted by an obsolete narrow-mindedness and incomprehensible rigidity. Youthful restiveness and the unwillingness to put up with familial and institutional restrictions increase by a quantum jump. Unease with formalized and organized interactions of all kinds also increases. This becomes one of the major dimensions of the reality gap. While *Newsweek* declares that "The Permissive Society" has arrived, much of middle-class youth experiences prying and intolerant stuffiness, while the freak experiences savage and brutal Puritanism. While liberals hail reform legislation as triumphs of the "democratic process," much of "straight" middle-class youth speaks somewhat negatively of "system" or "Establishment," and the freak lives in a military-bureaucratic-totalitarian police state ruled by "fascist pigs." All rules made by older people and authority figures tend therefore to be seen as alien and pointless contrivances.

The assumption that things-in-general have a "there-for-the-taking" quality desanctifies whatever authorities, institutions, and rules that happen to impede the spontaneous taking of whatever-it-is for purposes of personal satisfaction. Among conventional middle-class youth, this is reflected in the great increase in teen-age shopliftings in very recent years, mainly by girls between the ages of fifteen and seventeen whose fathers earn over $15,000 a year.

This kind of shoplifting, often encouraged by teen-age status competition and conformist pressures, evidently involves a mild personal freak-out on what is experienced as restrictively alien institutions, rules, and authority figures. Possibly, there are also indications here of feelings of nonexistence or powerlessness induced by the experience of having a discontinuous (and, in the "normal" teen-ager, largely submerged) reality *not taken seriously* by "adult" authority figures (and *all* older people are to some extent authority figures), especially the parents; the offspring resort (however unconsciously) to involving the parents in the objective consequences of action in accordance with the submerged other reality as it is permitted briefly to surface.

Even the "normal" and docile youths are therefore likely to display, on occasion, acute symptoms of conflict between a reality of experience that wells up from within and the conventional reality with which they are indoctrinated from without. But since their conscious interpretation of experience takes place within the conventional reality, the submerged reality will remain inchoate and will become less and less capable of modifying consciousness, as intellectual tools are developed to rationalize away disturbing thoughts and feelings. The individual gradually comes to feel what he believes. However, this becomes more difficult to accomplish with each successive youth generation; the attenuation of the Scarcity Principle breaks the motivational mainspring which causes individuals to accept with equanimity their roles within large-scale organizations. This leads to two main results: the desanctification of hierarchical authority, and a loss of interest in "achievement" and "goal-orientation."

This redirection of motivations will induce a feeling of being hemmed in by any structure which is not entirely created by oneself; which means by any structure in which anyone else is involved; which means by any structure, period. The feeling develops that all formal hierarchies are alien impositions which mutilate the self and disrupt the desired free flow of consciousness; they are somebody else's "trip." Just as the black lower-class youth feels that the ghetto is "colonized" by organizations and programs manipulated by whites from the Outside, so does the white middle-class youth come to feel that he is surrounded by structures which are manipulated from the Outside: they are not geared to his consciousness and therefore are in a sense "unreal." They are controlled by obsolete, irrelevant, absurdly dogmatic, brutal authorities who follow conveniently narrow and hypocritical interpretations of what they claim to be their own "values"—deluded old men; and they obstruct obvious and new possibilities of human growth by artificially and forcibly sustaining fixations on power and economic accumulation. While the white middle-class youths are certainly nowhere near as objectively deprived as people in the black lower class in the routine conditions of existence of their respective class environments, and are similarly far from being as objectively oppressed by routine and systematic brutality and terror, both groups nevertheless tend to experience subjectively in an *extreme form* the contradiction between the affluent society's possibilities and its fulfillments.

The vague sense of the unreality and oppressiveness of all the prevailing social institutions and culture that is experienced by middle-class youths is responded to by rock musicians, who are, we must remember, young people themselves and not the "tunesmiths" and song manufacturers of the "Tin Pan Alley" system who were much older than the mass public that consumed their products. The rock musician is generally under twenty-five years old and (as anyone can determine from a cursory inspection of album-cover photographs) is almost always a freak, with each new group trying to look and sound freakier than those preceding it. The enormous popularity of the music, and what appears to be an almost insatiable demand for ever more extreme expressions in sounds and lyrics, constitute the strongest possible proof of the continuity between freak-consciousness and the consciousness of the "straight" consuming public. Rock groups are in demand for such "square" events as fraternity and sorority dances (for which the "frat rats" will set up "psychedelic lights"), "pep rallies," and "after-the-game bashes." (The groups themselves will freely take of the System's money.) But, as already indicated, there are different levels on which the music is experienced.

In order to assure that the middle classes will consume compulsively, it is necessary to give them a reasonable certainty that they will not be overtaken by collective and, as far as possible, individual economic disaster. They will then assume a continuing burden of installment debt rather than "save for a rainy day"—it being understood that one can always get a loan in case of emergency. However, to their children, as indicated, growing up assuming the absolute certainty of the continuity of their physical well-being, even "chaos" and "anarchy" cease to be effective scare words. As also indicated, the accumulative motive, regarded in the middle classes as inseparable from present or future physical well-being, becomes attenuated; the accumulation of a given amount of money, possessions, power, high grades, status, etc., confers on the modal youth born into the middle- and upper-middle class less psychic gain than it would, say, on a youth born into the working or even lower-middle classes, in whom one might expect to find the Scarcity Principle more firmly implanted.

The psychic gain accruing to the middle-class youth from the successful performance of this entire inventory of interaction ritual, containing as it does a dimension of sublimated violence, and geared as it is to accumulative patterns of behavior such as the scramble for precedence, position, and selection in formal institutional contexts, comes to be reduced in its turn. It is regarded as a meaningless encumbrance, just like the "structures" and "system" of whose power it appears to be symptomatic. The establishment of social existence through appearance, popularity, possessions, membership in exclusive in-groups (such as college fraternities and sororities) recedes somewhat in importance, while a growing number of youths become convinced that the ritual behavior and criteria of superiority involve the futile degradation of the self and of others. Instead there develops a cult of emotional sophistication: "sensitivity," "beautiful person"-hood, being "real," "tenderness," "vulnerability," "inner freedom," being a "human being," "openness," being "loving," are some of the explicit personal ideals of this cult, which includes many who are very far from being freaks. On a collective level there is a hunger for "communication" and "community."

The rock musician's message is, over and over, and as we have already seen, to "look in yourself," "live your life behind your eyes," "dig yourself," "get into yourself." The objective is to discover a self which, supposedly, is untouched and unformed by the influences, pressures, and indoctrinations of organized society. This is what lies inside the "Gates of Eden." This is what The Beatles see when they turn off the lights that they know is theirs. Only this is to be considered "real" and the only truths and ideology to be taken seriously are those derived from "bringing it all back home" —exploring and developing this underlying self; and that knowledge which accords with what one has discovered from going through this process.

According to Dylan's version of this logic, traditional Marxists become those who, obsessed with "relationships of ownership," must compulsively "act accordingly and wait for succeeding kings"; they yearn to replace the existing authoritarian regime with one of their own. Meanwhile, "I try to harmonize with songs the lonesome sparrow sings / There are no kings inside the Gates of Eden." Academics and intellectuals avoid experience and are merely "paupers" who "change possessions each one wishing for what the other has got / While the princess and the prince discuss what is real and what is not." But, "It doesn't matter inside the Gates of Eden." Truths and realities are to be found in dreams and fantasies, which are to be accepted as they stand, without any attempt to interpret them through the use of standardized meanings and definitions, since this would lead one back into the universe of discourse of the conventional reality.

Quite often, the freaks do not succeed in escaping the stereotyping they so decry (as can be attested to by anyone who has observed their writing off of "straights," "squares," and so on as hopeless cases). And sometimes they are victims of their "freaky" world like this young man whose experiences in Washington fell considerably short of freak expectations:

Dear Free Press:

I can't see anybody's feelings getting hurt by lonely little me. And should not one better concept in this tirade come as news to the "love people" of D.C. but since I hit Washington, I have been impressed with the sickness here that soaks the hopeless souls in every level of society and not-society.

I have canned and conned and hassled till I have caught the sickness again. I'm crying like a two-timed teenybopper now.

Mr. Graybusinesssuit, half-man of governmental and corporate bureaucracy, has played the company game so dynamically that folks like me are on the run from the draft, from the heat [police] and from the unfreedom. The sickness is not too subtle—you think about it when the cops drag down their stupid, arbitrary statutes to make you fall in, you think about it when you dig the morning paper, *Life* magazine, and the TV set, when your old man disowns you, and old ladies glare at you out of their cashmere. And the sick-news is sick on a big scale. I've found it in every corner of the country from Pocatello to Portland, in the rah-rah two party ilk of election year. I've spent my short years of turned on-ness building my own freaky defenses against it.

And, praise goodness, honesty, love, trust, freedom and the human spirit, there were always folks who spoke my language, cried my teardrops and shared my dope [marijuana].

I travel a lot. Until I came to D.C. I never had to beg on the streets, sleep in bus terminals until evicted, get hassled over employment shirks, or talk to myself when I needed company. I lived such an unshaven, smelly clothing life for two weeks until I could make enough of their goddamned money to where people would actually talk to me.

Oh life is rough and people are mostly unkind, but this need not be. Freaks always knew that and freaks set out to live at folks so that the old vision of love and trust didn't die. But in D.C., don't ask me how, the freaks took my little stake and let me off at fear again, and I just wasn't ready for that.

Now I accept your apology and your explanation that if I'd found the right folks it would have been different. I want to ask the right folks. Where the hell they are?

At any rate, I'm still alive and able to leave here with my health, and I have learned my lesson. But one thing burns in me, and I have to ask: where's it going to end freaks? Shall we keep on accepting the colossal burn that we are pulling on each other? Do you want to spread the American sickness, with a D.C. twist, or do you want to destroy it?

The spaces are conning and being conned and being subtly bought and rebought three blocks from anywhere. Whose side are you on anyway? We've got to start pulling together before we all strangle in this soul-starvation. The man and his game are getting out of hand, getting a rotten finger in our heads. I suggest we say a far, emphatic "FUCK YOU" to it. Time's a wastin'. Let's start digging ourselves at all levels and maybe salvage our lives from all this shit.

LOVE,
Stephen Harris

P.S. Hiding don't do no good, a man's got to live with his head!

What lies within the "Gates of Eden," then, is this: Feeling is Truth. And since feeling derives from new configurations of motivation and personality, what is accepted as knowledge in the conventional reality comes to be "felt" as lies. Formal education, in the words of a nineteen-year-old girl hanging around Marshall Street in Syracuse, is no more than "putting things in boxes." The box is a figure used by dissident middle-class youth in imagery associated with feelings of intense disgust: suburban houses are "little boxes"; automobiles are "metal boxes." The revulsion at straight-line aesthetics also appears in the derogatory use of such words as "straight" and "square." McLuhan is surely correct when he warns of the obsolescence of categorization methods of subdividing and imparting knowledge, and of the necessity to accompany the imparting of knowledge with "depth experience" and training in "pattern recognition." For their part, drug-culture intellectuals and freak-radicals have eagerly assimilated McLuhan's theories; contributing to this popularity is McLuhan's seeming playfulness ("None of my books should be taken seriously.")

Youth-cultural manifestations are full of being stifled and manipulated. Yet they are often accompanied, sometimes in immediate juxtaposition, by expressions of (seemingly antithetical feelings of) complete freedom and independence from social pressures and authoritarian domination, as well as of the transcendence of the mundane world of petty rules, regulations, and organizational constraints. Within the same consciousness, therefore, the experience of the social universe can precipitate either a depressed and helpless feeling of total imprisonment or a joyous—"groovy" —feeling of total freedom. There is no contradiction; these are opposite sides of the same coin.

The individual *shares* a middle-class youth subculture with others whose basic personality configurations are similar because of common historical experience. Meanwhile, he lives in the midst of organized institutions which have objectively been rendered structurally obsolete because of the abundance of things-in-general actually produced; the social utility of repressive and hierarchical-authoritarian structural arrangements declines to the degree that is unnecessary to regulate the distribution of the surplus in a subsistence economy or to spur the accumulation of the means of production in an industrializing economy.

As indicated, the youth consistently and, to some extent, consciously experiences organized society as incompatible with, or in contradiction to, what he is aware of as his most authentic and "natural" impulses and inclinations; his youth culture validates his discontents and assists in refining and focusing them. As this consciousness develops, organized society comes to be felt as a clever conspiracy for humiliating, smothering, castrating, manipulating, and possibly even killing him. The more his subjectivity is intensified, the more he feels confronted by a monolithic array of the forces of death intent on the suppression of sex, love, life, beauty, freedom, insight, untapped psychic powers, being, depth, peace, joy, music, novelty, sensory experience—everything summed up or implied by the word "groovy." The more repressive he senses the social universe to be, the greater his feelings of powerlessness and insignificance in relation to it. Psychic operations and social interaction within the universe of discourse of the conventional reality become pointless, depressing, or a species of torment: "a drag," or "a real down."

By contrast, the more the youth becomes aware of his subjective reality the more the exploration and intensification of it becomes desirable for its own sake and without need of further justification—other than the belief that "You're more real when you're high." Immersion in the subjective reality may appear to provide an understanding or vision of what is wrong with "this fucked-up world," which transcends the concepts and meaning with which communication is standardized within the universe of discourse of the conventional reality. This subjective world also provides the youth with what he thinks are new powers: he can abolish seemingly irrelevant distinctions, think "inconceivable" thoughts, and derive a guide for "inconceivable" actions. His means of evasion of and resistance to what seem to be oppressive environmental conditions and a miscellany of obtuse people are drastically extended. He enjoys himself ever more profoundly, overcomes loneliness, and counteracts his feelings of powerlessness and insignificance. What he finds inside the "Gates of Eden" provides him with what rings true as the authentic response to the social universe which he actually experiences; and he must believe in it or be spiritually crushed. One is reminded of some of the slogans on buttons worn by the hippies: "Nirvana Now!" or "Reality is a nice place to visit, but I wouldn't want to live there."

CHAPTER 9

The Freak Versus "The System"

Unlike the self-consciously defeated "beat generation" of the late fifties, who were reconciled to the permanent status of an insignificant minority, the freaks of the sixties construed themselves as the Wave of the Future. They had messianic tendencies; they wanted to "turn on" or "radicalize" everyone to "where it's at."

The main thrust of hippieism lay in the direction of what the freak musician Ed Sanders (leader of The Fugs; in 1968, one of the five principal "nonleaders" of the yippies) called a "total assault on the culture." This assault obviously included the adoption of all sorts of behavior, apparel, and speech known to be offensive to the "straights." More broadly, the hippies undermined the culture through the annihilation of meanings, the scrambling of communication, and the repudiation of culturally accepted principles of causality. Hippies would have recourse to spells, incantations, hexagrams, "cosmic mind force"; the impact of this was to bewilder the "straights" to the point of asking the inevitable question, "What do you hope to *accomplish* by doing this?" Freaks reply to this question with giggles, cross-eyed stares, or perhaps a lecture on the "accomplishment hang-up" which continues until the freak realizes that *he* is trying to accomplish something and then withdraws to groove on the contradiction. Freak behavior generally appears to the "straight" mind as random, maddeningly whimsical, and disgustingly devoid of concerted effort of any kind; large numbers of freaks will, in good weather, sprawl miscellaneously over the sidewalk, cavort in the middle of the street oblivious to traffic, and, in general, infest an environment to the obstruction and hindrance of purposeful effort and gainful commerce.

Let it be stressed that the culturally subversive practices engaged in by freaks are, for the most part, neither readily classifiable nor discretely isolable within the general context of the freak lifestyle. It is never possible to disentangle the urge to amuse the cultural insiders from the desire to confuse the cultural outsiders. Nor is it always possible to determine whether the "straights" are regarded as prospective converts whose involuntary involvement would break down their defenses, or whether they are regarded as hopeless cases whose neutralization is a sufficient achievement. In this context, it should be pointed out that the freak does not regard himself as a member of a creative elite condemned by its sensitivity to perpetual minority status and political impotence. Instead, he believes that his subculture is at the very least a proxy for the youth of the entire society; ultimately (preferably, of course, NOW!) everyone will be "turned on."

Disorientation becomes a political weapon, as is indicated by the malicious glee with which blacks and freaks inflict *symbolic pollution* upon the objects, institutions, and physical premises of the "Establishment." Black lower-class people disturb the bourgeois stuffiness of official meetings and other environments with loud singing, cursing, and "telling it like it is" in ghetto language; Hamilton Hall at Columbia is renamed Malcolm X University; radical white middle-class youth smoke pot on the steps of the Pentagon; Diggers throw burning dollar bills from the gallery of the New York Stock Exchange. Once more the French student slogans are instructive: "I am a Marxist of the Groucho tendency," "Rape your alma mater," and "Invent a new sexual perversion." The symbolic pollution is a deliberate, forced juxtaposition of antithetical meanings; it is the unprecedented doing of the culturally inadmissible.

Weapons of cultural aggression are commonly conceptualized

by freaks by the use of such terms as the *put-on,* the *goof,* and the *mind-fuck.*

In a put-on, the freak indulges his fantasy while taking advantage of the straight's credulity and fear of the unknown. The freak thoroughly enjoys the situation and celebrates his own weirdness; any panic or bewilderment which he may induce contributes to his satisfaction but is not central. He is being aggressively himself and is disseminating a wish fulfillment derived directly from his subjective reality; it is therefore not *entirely* correct to say that he is "lying" or "kidding"—he does not operate according to "realistic expectations." In a celebrated instance, a hippie candidate in the April 1967 election for the Berkeley, California, City Council had himself officially designated on the ballot as a "Wandering Priest." During the campaign he promised that if elected he would open an "LSD temple" in the city, making the initial disclosure of this project in the offices of the Berkeley *Gazette* (the local "Establishment" newspaper). The paper, while treating the whole thing as a joke, nevertheless broke the story (January 31, 1967) with a front-page banner headline. At the very least, large numbers of citizens were thus confronted with alien thought patterns. ("I am a holy man, seeking Eternal Truth, following a Law far higher than the laws our government passes upon us. . . .") But who is to say that he would not have delivered on his campaign promises had he won?

Even better known, because of national media coverage, is an escapade of June 1968, in which a number of San Francisco hippies, claiming to be convinced of the imminence of the Apocalypse in the form of the asteroid Icarus colliding with the Earth, fled to the Colorado Rockies to await the End of the World in a peaceful and spiritually inspiring primitive setting. There were simultaneous prophecies of catastrophic earthquakes in California due to a complete slippage along the San Andreas Fault: "California is going to break away from the continent and drop off into the Pacific Ocean." (Ted Zatlyn, "Apocalypse," *Los Angeles Free Press,* June 7, 1967.)

While none of these disasters occurred, and by all accounts a good time was had by all, it is also true that the various prophets in question *did* believe (and no doubt still do) that the existing order of things is doomed, or at least deserves to be:

And California—haven't we witnessed in the last two years its breakaway from the rest of the country? The love revolution found its magnetic center in San Francisco and Los Angeles; for thousands of people last summer it became the place to break away from an old life style, from an old age worn out with wars, with materiality, deceit and corruption and bloodshed.

If the state is to slip into the Pacific—will it not be an actualization of a thought shared by those who already separated themselves not out of a lust for gold, but out of a hunger to understand themselves and the coming age? (*Ibid.*)

Put-ons vary according to the degree of direct involvement of and malevolence toward the "straights." At one extreme is the sort of prank rumor with which freaks put each other on and which gets taken seriously by the "straights," who then comically demonstrate their gullibility and stupidity. In this category are such things as "The Great Banana Hoax" of 1967, when the word was spread that one could get mildly (and legally) high by smoking powdered, dried, banana peel. This resulted in all sorts of hilarious consternation among the "straights"; government scientists, for instance, rushed madly about trying to isolate the nonexistent hallucinogenic substance. At the other extreme is the deliberate "hype," often addressed to officials or members of the press which, while it is recognized for what it is by the in-group, is intended to induce panic and overreaction in the ranks of the cultural-political enemy. The New York City yippies, for example, threatened (June 1968) a "riot" in St. Marks Place and a "loot-in" in Macy's. Abbie Hoffman, a yippie "nonleader" and quintessential freak, is credited with remarkable successes in Chicago in August:

> Hoffman, not incidentally, is a past member of the art of "hype" in talking to the press. Shortly after his arrival, he announced blandly that Yippies would put LSD in the city's water supply; Chicago immediately put a guard on to watch its entire water system. When, after the Yippie pig was busted in Civic Center, Hoffman made the deadpan announcement that "next time we're going to nominate a lion," the guard was doubled at Lincoln Park Zoo. ("The Decline and Fall of the Democratic Party," *Ramparts*, September 28, 1968.)

The highest form of *goof,* from which the greatest amusement is derived, is a *prank* that results in the straight becoming disconcerted or confused or else incited to overreact or fall back on self-defeating stupid and primitive behavior; the straight's cultural assumptions are ridiculed, defied, and undermined in the process. Playful prankishness is a basic freak style; the novelist Ken Kesey's prototypical hippie tribe, which flourished in 1965, was called The Merry Pranksters.

Some recent illustrative events:

In August (1968), a Marshall Street freak, working as a short-order cook in a restaurant, told me that "A bunch of freaks were walking up the street ahead of the meter maid and putting nickels in meters so she couldn't write out tickets. Finally she got upset and yelled at them, "You dirty weirdos! Why don't you get a job!" So one of them says, "I have a job—putting nickels in parking meters."

A friend of mine who is an associate Professor in the Syracuse University School of Social Work tells me that in July a hairy freak had come by his office for a visit "without an appointment." When informed by the secretary that "Mr. F—— is not in" (which was true) the freak reportedly proceeded to calmly light up a joint and take a few tokes. My friend says that, upon smelling the marijuana smoke, all the faculty and secretaries in the building were thrown into a complete panic. To the best of anyone's knowledge, this was the first time that anyone had actually committed a Social Problem on the premises of the Syracuse University School of Social Work.

Since freaks get infuriated by middle-class tourists who regard them as packaged entertainment to be consumed, it is only natural that this goof should have happened:

60 HIPPIES IN A BUS SEE THE SIGHTS OF QUAINT QUEENS

A group of East Village hippies who became annoyed with the increasing number of tourist buses visiting St. Marks Place turned the tables with a vengeance yesterday.

Sixty of them, camera straps tangled with the beads around their necks, paid $5 apiece and boarded a rented Greyhound bus for a midday sightseeing tour of Queens. . . .

For four hours, the bus cruised along the borough's thoroughfares and sidestreets as the hippies stared through their dark glasses at housing developments, bowling alleys and supermarkets, the middle-class landmarks they had forsaken but not forgotten. . . .

During a stop in Jamaica Estates, the sightseers walked up and down the sedate, tree-lined blocks, staring at the residents who were watering their lawns and reading the Sunday papers.

"Hey, what do you do at night around here?" a hippie asked Mrs. Margot Kuchenmeister, of 11 181st Street, whose grandson, Gerald, had run into the two-story brick house to fetch his camera.

"Not much," she said. "We go to sleep early. What do you do?"

Her question went unanswered, as the group filed back to the bus and then traveled back to Manhattan, humming on kazoos that had been passed around.

On Second Avenue the bus overtook another bus, also filled with tourists on its way to the Village. (*The New York Times,* September 23, 1968.)

Five days later the *Times* reported another cultural clash, this one more overtly political. Freak-radical students "representing the C.C.N.Y. commune, Students for a Democratic Society and the Youth International Party (yippies)" materialized at Lewisohn Stadium, where City College's Reserve Officers Training Corps unit was holding an early-morning drill:

RADICALS "TAKE ON" CADETS

About 75 radical students from City College had a glorious time doing their "thing" yesterday morning, which was to mock an equal number of R.O.T.C. cadets doing their "thing"—namely, drilling.

For two hours the students skipped, danced, scampered and tumbled around the cadets, like a swarm of gnats. Half the cadets, with ever-straight faces, practiced marching drills and the others ran obstacle courses and races. . . .

The radicals' demonstrations started somewhat hesitantly at first, at 8 A.M. on the dust-covered field at Lewisohn Stadium.

"Brothers!" called a long-haired youth over a public address box. "Frisbee classes are now beginning in Lewisohn Stadium. You people in R.O.T.C., we're getting some orange juice. You're welcome to have some and join us."

Red, white and blue frisbees began to soar on one half of the field while a group of cadets stood at attention on the other. . . .

It was 8:30 as a second group of about 25 cadets ran across the field, dressed in fatigues, to an area laid out with hurdles and taped lines.

"It's all yours," shouted a student leader. "Let's march in our nonmilitary way and take it." They followed the cadets in fatigues and from then on, had a field day.

They somersaulted over each other, played leap frog, waved

their arms in amorphous dances, and raced with the cadets who
were crawling, running and jumping obstacle courses.

The radicals excelled in this phase of their antiwar demonstration, which they called "A Celebration of Life."

They joined in a drill where the cadets raced carrying other
cadets on their backs, in fireman fashion.

The civilian students came in first, second, third, and fifth
among four other teams made up of cadets.

They lampooned the cadets continuously, marching behind
them, running in front of them, shouting slogans.

The black flag of anarchy appeared and was used to lead cadets
running around the field track. (*The New York Times,* September
28, 1968.)

The mind fuck, as the phrase obviously implies, is a deliberate
attempt to shock, infuriate, confuse, or terrorize the "straights" by
perpetrating inconceivable weirdness upon them. It is expected
that the "straights" will not take it in good humor but will rather
"blow their cool"—although the freaks will themselves be having
a good laugh unless they are arrested. This normally involves the
wholesale violation of rules and canons of polite behavior, dress,
and language; it is an eruption of an intensified version of the freak
life-style into environments where the "straights" are supposedly
secure.

The use of symbolic pollution has already been discussed.
More serious forms of psycho-terror involve the invasion, desecra-
tion, disruption, or occupation of enemy environments. Guerrilla
artists in San Francisco steal out in the dead of night to paint what
they consider to be ugly and boring institutional environments.
The Guerrilla Theater in Washington, D.C., stages "surprise attacks." In New York City, Kusama's "liberated women" perpe-
trate guerrilla nudity in such places as Wall Street, the Statue of
Liberty, and United Nations Plaza. Freaks have urinated and
painted four-letter words on the walls of the Pentagon and have
celebrated the Vernal Equinox en masse in the lobby of Grand
Central Station.

Basic to the mind-fuck is the freak's horror of anything which
is "plastic"—shiny-smooth, bland-textured, emotionally unde-
manding, machine-tooled, unabrasive, mass-produced, precision-
prefabricated, neat, clean products of mass consumption. The
freak will, generally speaking, condemn as "plastic" anything and

anybody smacking of the mass culture and the suburban way of life. This especially includes diluted versions of freak-culture manifestations which are intended to be sold in the mass market-place to fad-minded consumers; persons who adopt the freak life-style in a superficial and inane fashion; and youthful-looking "Establishment" figures, such as the late Senator Robert F. Kennedy, whose efforts to "establish communication" or "open a dialogue with youth" are regarded as cynically manipulative.

That which is "plastic" represents an avoidance or distortion of all that the freak regards as "life" and "reality"; it is a hallucination. For example, consider a singing group called Up With People, organized by Moral Re-Armament with funds supplied by Patrick Frawley, the reactionary multimillionaire owner of Schick, Inc. It is intended to be a wholesome, clean-cut, well-scrubbed counter-force ("Not a hippie among them!") to rock music and other freak-culture manifestations of which its patrons disapprove. (If I were a vulgar Marxist I would jump to the conclusion that the sales of Frawley's razors are potentially imperiled by the freaks' predilection for facial hair.) Up With People gave a concert in the Syracuse War Memorial in late April 1968; a local freak responded to this incursion of "cheap acetate" by distributing hundreds of copies of this leaflet:

UP WITH PEOPLE

ABSOLUTE HONESTY

They will—with the honesty and integrity of a modern day president—answer *all* your questions on Asia, Africa, Latin and South America, communism, capitalism, imperialism, fascism, and freedom.

ABSOLUTE UNSELFISHNESS

Why, they must be *communists*!!

ABSOLUTE PURITY

These fine Americans are pure—absolutely pure—no crimes, no guilt, no evil associations, they do not fuck or masturbate—there are no blackheads on their noses—no dirt underneath their toenails—no hemorrhoids, no vaginitis, no crotch rot, not a necrophiliac among them. No latent homosexuals—never a thought of cunnilingus. They are absolutely pure.

ABSOLUTE LOVE

Watch these 35 young Americans—feel their absolute love—their love for people and the American way—feel their love for the burned babies and soldiers of Vietnam—feel their love for the millions of Vietnamese people who are starving and rotting in refugee camps while U.S. soldiers fuck their women—feel their compassion for the 30 million imprisoned blacks of southern Africa—hear their love manifest itself in songs of praise for U.S. police and national guardsmen who beat and club and MACE and pump 20 bullets into 17 year old black Bobby Hutton who came out with his hands over his head to surrender—surrender to death of the American way—observe their sympathy for the 2,700 political prisoners of Greece who are being tortured while a party for the military junta is being held on a U.S. ship only minutes away—listen to songs of praise and joy and love for Missouri fire department which lets houses burn down because residents have not yet paid their $7 fee for their fire protection tag—Yes, come, see, feel and hear absolute love——

A few months later the Syracuse University SDS activists tried to counteract the organized inanities of the September "Orientation Week" by distributing a "Disorientation Handbook" to the entering freshmen. The front cover of this document features a caption, "Chancellor Tolley and Hubert Humphrey," which serves for two pictures. The first is a photograph of the Syracuse University Chancellor and the Democratic presidential nominee in full academic regalia. The second is a drawing of a pair of copulating rats. The chancellor, in a speech welcoming the freshman class, is said to have accused the radicals of lacking a "sense of humor."

Another variant of the mind-fuck is the celebration of acts regarded with horror by more conventional people. Consider, for example, one freak reaction to the attempted murder of Andy Warhol, the "pop artist" and film-maker, who is despised by freak-intellectuals as the personification of the celebrity system—the product of publicity, image-building, and being defined as "in" by other celebrities. When Warhol was shot by Valerie Solanas, a minor member of his entourage and the author of the lesbian-feminist *S.C.U.M.* (Society for Cutting Up Men) *Manifesto,* the freak-revolutionary commune Up Against the Wall Motherfucker ("THE FUTURE OF OUR STRUGGLE IS THE FUTURE OF CRIME IN THE STREETS . . .") responded by distributing the following leaflet:

ANDY WARHOL SHOT BY VALERIE SOLANAS. PLASTIC MAN VS. THE SWEET ASSASSIN—THE FACE OF PLASTIC /FASCIST SMASHED—THE TERRORIST KNOWS WHERE TO STRIKE—AT THE HEART—A RED PLASTIC INEVIT-

ABLE EXPLODED—NON-MAN SHOT BY THE REALITY OF HIS DREAM (AS THE CULTURAL ASSASSIN EMERGES)—A TOUGH LITTLE CHICK—THE "HATER" OF MEN AND THE LOVER OF MAN—WITH THE SURGEON'S GUN—NOW—AGAINST THE WALL OF PLASTIC EXTINCTION—AN EPOXY NIGHTMARE WITH A DEAD SUPERSTAR—THE STATUE OF LIBERTY RAPED BY A CHICK WITH BALLS—THE CAMP MASTER SLAIN BY THE SLAVE—AND AMERICA'S WHITE PLASTIC CATHEDRAL IS READY TO BURN. VALERIE IS OURS AND THE SWEET ASSASSIN LIVES.   (*East Village Other,* July 5, 1968.)

The late Senator Robert F. Kennedy was often associated—in terms of "image"—with the same "pop"-celebrity milieu that spawned Warhol. Following his assassination (June 5, 1968), a Syracuse freak took to praising the accused killer Sirhan B. Sirhan as "the people's assassin." When Senator Edwin S. Muskie, the Democratic vice-presidential nominee, delivered a campaign speech (which was badly disrupted by heckling) at Syracuse University, this young man shouted, "Free all political prisoners like Sirhan!"

Yet another variant of the mind-fuck derives from the freak's horror of "plastic situations" (institutionally packaged, with streamlined exteriors masking shoddy and bland contents). These can include organizational meetings and conventions; high school and college classes; conversations wtih "straights," such as bureaucrats or the parents of one's sex partner; job environments; or contacts with representatives of the mass media. The neat, orderly, and etiquette-laden behavior demanded in such situations appears to the freak not only as unbearably stuffy but also as conducive to intolerable authoritarianism, and (worst of all) to the acceptance of the universe of discourse of the conventional reality, which is a hallucinatory denial of reality as the freak experiences it. The freak's impulse is either to escape or to smash the rules and thereby recreate the spontaneous interaction and fuller emotional expression that prevail on the street. Imagine, therefore, a televised panel discussion featuring three representatives of the "underground" media, and moderated (freaks having no use for moderation of any kind) by a reporter from *The New York Times* (which in a sense *is* the conventional reality, upper-middle-class liberal version).

Reality was performed on Channel 13, WNDT-TV, Tuesday night, June 25th, at 10:30 P.M. A live reenactment of chaos sent shock waves through the New York metropolitan area as thousands of viewers witnessed the first physical confrontation between the underground and the establishment media. What was happening in Paris, in Vietnam, in Berlin, in Tokyo, in practically every major city in the world was happening at that exact moment on the third eye of living-room consciousness: REBELLION.

It was to be a calm discussion of "The Meaning of the Underground Press," with Jeff Shero from *The Rat,* Marvin Fishman from Underground Newsreel [a New Left documentary film-making commune], and "Yours truly" from the *East Village Other,* along with Steve Roberts, *New York Times* correspondent, as M.C.

Roberts had just finished asking the first question after our introductions, and Jeff Shero was about to give the first answer, when loud banging on the studio's doors and muffled shouts merged into the studio and spilled into a pile of twenty-five people among the three TV cameras and ten crewmen. In an instant the studio was transformed into a low-budget *War and Peace* with a 50 x 30 foot area as a battlefield. "The enemy" was dressed, as all media people from the underground are, with beards, books, beads, sandals, one indian headband, cameras, motion picture cameras and tape-recorders. This was the meaning of the Underground Press.

All of a sudden, everyone started to speak at once:
"GET OUT. YOU DON'T BELONG HERE!"
"WE WERE INVITED!"
"WHO ARE YOU?"
"WE'RE THE UNDERGROUND PRESS!"
Tower of Babel was suddenly reenacted before the TV camera's eyes. The establishment media in the guise of Steve Roberts asked reasons and the underground media in the guise of Marvin Fishman echoed back questions.

"Why can't they do this?" shouted Fishman. "They have every right to be here. They're the Underground Press!" pointing at the twenty odd people actively standing around taking pictures, tape recording, letting the cameras roll and asking their questions:
"WHY DOES TV HAVE TO BE YOUR WAY?"
"WHY IS THE ESTABLISHMENT MEDIA ALWAYS LYING?"
"WHY CAN'T WE CHANGE THE FORM OF THE SHOW?"
The questions seemed to all fall on Roberts as he became the central focus of all their inquiries. He sat there, his jaw locked on twenty voices at the same time as mental sweat plainly visible rolled down his flushed face.

But in the underground media's haste to pinpoint the enemy they forgot to protect their rear as other establishment troops behind them had kept the TV cameras turned on them. Suddenly the battle turned into a battle of the cameras as underground newsreel people turned, reeled and shot footage at the TV cameramen shooting back.

Before anyone knew it, Marvin Fishman was saying, "Why can't we say FUCK on the air." And as if to answer his own rhetorical question, "FUCK THE ESTABLISHMENT." . . .

Suddenly the atmosphere changed as Marvin Fishman realized that Channel 13 had called the police. Everyone started to retreat to the studio doors. Jeff Shero stood up and announced, "If they leave, I must leave." I got up last and didn't say anything but remembered the old adage, "The underground media may have its beliefs but the Establishment has the bullets."

We retreated through the studio door as the TV people, assistant director, programmer, script girl, private TV policeman, stalked our tracks out onto the main floor. When we exited out onto the streets, some fat middle-aged women with "yenta" voices, started shouting at us. *"You bums you!"* The police at that exact moment drove up and the women started shouting, *"Here they are."* . . . The police caught about eight people as the rest just split into different directions and vanished without the police realizing there were more. I stood there and watched the police taking the eight back to the TV station to find out what was going on. I followed and entered the station with them. Jeff Shero, who was also among us, and I were excused from the arrest because, as the studio put it, "We were invited guests." The others were charged with assault . . . trespassing and various other sundries, including burglary and riot. Bob Ferrero, the planner of the show on underground newspapers asked me if I had known about it beforehand. I told him "NO." It turned out later that Jeff Shero had not known about it either. As for Marvin, we couldn't ask him as he was one of the swifter ones who had made into the night. . . . I had joined the eight others because I now felt their arrest was wrong. They didn't, in my mind, deserve the type of punishment that was meted out to them, only bad ratings. The studio overacted like children when they should have known the children whom nobody leads are the children who know they are children. They overacted but we were only acting. The same war we waged in that studio Tuesday night was the same war the establishment wages in Vietnam. . . .

(Allan Katzman in *East Village Other,* July 5, 1968.)

I have quoted this piece at such length because it is a highly characteristic specimen of "underground" journalism: emotional meanings are much more significant to the writer than a detailed recounting of the "facts." What might appear to outsiders as "logical contradictions" (e.g., the writer's fantasy of himself as a guerrilla warrior and, in the same breath, his complaint that the station was being unfair—an amazing juxtaposition, insofar as he must have been exposed to Ernesto "Che" Guevara's maxim, "In revolution one wins or dies.") are apparently nonexistent in the writer's subjective reality.

The WNDT-TV staff no doubt conceived of themselves as a group of advanced-thinking creative types (which they certainly *are,* by the standards set by the other six VHF stations serving New York City) who were being what is called "relevant" by giving the viewing audience some sanitized exposure to three far-out deviants who, moreover, might be good for a few laughs. The freaks, as is the custom for spokesmen of powerless minorities, were expected to feel honored by the opportunity to present "their side" on television. But the editors and their friends, as children of the Electronic Age, were not "hung up" by the magical aspects of televised communication (as are most other people in this society). The station was just another institution in the grip of an Alien Power. Accordingly (as maintained in the "Panelists Statement" signed by Fishman, Katzman, and Shero), what took place was "an attempt by members of the underground community to inject authenticity into a sterilized and stultifying program format." The consequences served to reinforce the assumptions about social causality that are implicit in their shared subcultural reality: "It was just at that point when WNDT was confronted existentially with an opportunity to present the real underground that it chose to call the police."

On a deeper cultural level, the street freaks might be said to flout outrageously the American taboo on conspicuously doing nothing in public. To the casual observer, the directly visible features of street life seem to consist mainly of hanging around, sitting around, milling around, and lying around; knots of people form and dissolve; people crouch against walls, lean against cars, or cluster together and talk. A minority will be panhandling, hawking underground newspapers, scrawling designs or graffiti on the pavement, listening to rock music on transistor radios, caressing or engaging in sexual horseplay, making flimsy sculptures out of odds and ends of garbage, unaccountably giggling and spewing incoherent babble, or pointing movie cameras at everyone else. The casual "straight" observer, who is perhaps watching all this from the window of an air-conditioned sight-seeing bus, can detect very little that he considers to be of much social utility; nor much more that appears related to any organized, coordinated, and time-binding activities; nor can he easily identify activities which he can readily associate with his notions about "achievement drives." He observes, generally speaking, practically nothing that he can call "productive" within the limits of the various meanings which he attaches to this word. He is either outraged or titillated; possibly both. He may denounce "parasites" and "lazy bums" or else find comfort in the pseudoscientific gibberish employed by those hack writers who, in describing the supposed evil effects of marijuana, refer to a "significant reduction in social productivity," and an "emotivational syndrome." When the stereotype freak panhandles this stereotype "straight" on the street, asking the ritual question, "Got any spare change?" he gets the ritual reply, as if by conditioned reflex, "Why don't you get a job!"

At the other extreme, freaks will commonly work on a casual basis ("to pick up some bread") at jobs so idiotically routine that the tasks can be performed without interfering with the desired free flow of subjectivity; e.g., the freak can work while stoned. A classic example of this was the San Francisco Post Office's reliance on hippie labor to sort mail (with an occasional letter getting stamped USE EROGENOUS ZONE NUMBERS).

Coming back to the street or small park filled with freaks languorously muttering, "What's happening, man?" "Nothing, man.": For the reasons suggested above, they are not inclined to try to legitimatize their doing nothing in public as "recreation," "leisure-time activities," "study breaks," "recharging my batteries," or any of the other rationalizations considered acceptable by the dominant culture, all involving the general principle of "Even when I'm doing nothing, I feel that I'm doing something," as a Syracuse University undergraduate put it. The ideologically consistent freak will reject the very concept of "doing" as opposed to "being." He will flaunt the seeming aversion to "work" in the faces of the "straights," as, for example, does Tuli Kupferberg of the Fugs, who wrote a book called *1001 Ways to Live Without Working*. Street freaks have experimented with highly imaginative forms of public indolence, as in Haight-Ashbury in 1967, ". . . where, if you are a hippie and you have a dime, you can put it in a parking meter and lie down in the street for an hour's suntan (30 minutes for a nickel) and most drivers will be careful not to run you over." (Warren Hinckle, "A Social History of the Hippies," *Ramparts,* March 1967.)

As I have already said, the degree to which the energies of individuals are harnessed directly or indirectly to the fulfillment of the goals of large-scale organizations is *objectively* of rapidly declining social utility—granted that it may be impossible to determine the optimum point. That portions of the American economy are *objectively* describable as "organized waste" is a proposition subject to extensive disputation, with the exception of the undeniable fact that these portions are enormous. And it is *objectively* true that the existing class hierarchy is maintained at least in part through the practice of genocide and racism.

Subjectively and—usually—nebulously, the freak senses the cumulative and compounding irrationalities and, unlike the "straights" of his own age, is no longer able or willing to suppress the patterns he thinks he recognizes from his consciousness. The straights are much too crazy for him to "function" in their midst. Repelled by organizational life, he de-emphasizes his investment of energy ("libidinal cathexis" if you like) in those mechanisms and areas of personality which are useful within organizational contexts (and that means all organizational contexts, with the exception of the most fluid and anarchic). In his hierarchy of motives, less significance comes to be attached to "problem-solving" and "task-oriented" faculties; the setting and actualizing of goals, the sensitivity to status and role patterns in institutionally packaged situations, the culturally standardized sense of time together with the reliance on the clock for the orderly regulation of daily life, "neatness-orderliness-cleanliness" in the presentation of self, "achievement" and "competitive" drives, and what are conventionally regarded as "orderly" and "logical" thought processes. Energies are diverted to exploring, complicating, and exhibiting the self; searching for the immediate gratification of sexual and other cravings; expressing, communicating to others, and immediately acting on one's most intense feeling without modulation or self-censorship; becoming immersed in the depth experience of all sorts of environmental stimuli, ranging from the textures of objects to the emotions and states of consciousness of other people; and devising new defense mechanisms ("cool") which can prevent the personality from being torn apart as a result of the impact of powerful pressures and shocks to which it is deliberately exposed. The latter personality configuration abandons the "Reality Principle" (acquiescence to controls set by repressive forces in the environment as a necessity to ensure the survival of the individual) and, in the limiting case, would operate entirely in accordance with the "Pleasure Principle" (expecting the immediate and effortless fulfillment of wishes for the gratification of instinctual and other needs). Personalities tending in this direction are conventionally classified as "narcissistic" and are regarded as immature and childish.

"Repressive culture fosters immaturity. It cradles the ego in vinyl upholstery and shields it with tinted windshield glass. . . . Life slithers among us as an alien thing . . ." ("Good News," *Washington Free Press,* May 31, 1968.)

But the "Reality Principle," as it applies to the acquisition of higher-order motives, is in large measure the implantation in the personality of the Scarcity Principle in the culture. Classical psychoanalytic theory, starting with Freud, held that it was essential for society to repress human instincts in order to organize production and regulate the distribution of scarce output; only this made civilization possible. This in turn legitimatized the efforts of parents, authorities, and therapists to induce the individual to "face reality." It was never contemplated that a society would arise so rich that a highly visible minority of its youth would find the acquisition of material possessions to be a rather measly reward in exchange for the repressions they are required to undergo; who suspect, on the basis of the reality of their everyday lives, that these repressions are systematically and substantively insane; and who derive from drug experiences satisfactions and illuminations which reconfirm the reality of experience beyond the point where it can be affected by the pleadings of parents, the threats of authorities, and the "help" and tranquilizers of therapists.

The "Reality Principle," for the freaked-out personality, becomes partially collapsed into the "Pleasure Principle," since the freak ideally "digs himself" and can "groove" on almost anything. He consciously strives to achieve a state of childlike purity, magical transcendence, or "holy innocence," free from the cynical corruptions of the parental generation. He is born again as a Whole New Thing, experiencing everything anew and exclaiming "Beautiful!", "Groovy!" and the childlike cry of wonder, "Oh wow!" And Bob Dylan, having abandoned the composition of "protest" songs for the Old New Left to explore the creative possibilities of freak-consciousness, announced that "I was so much older then, / I'm younger than that now." [1]

In the limiting case, therefore, the freak tends to resist doing anything which has any reason for being done other than the sheer doing of it. Ideally, he would like to get paid for just living (i.e., "doing his Thing").

The freak's conspicuous cultural aggression, based on his "nonproductive" life style, is routinely challenged on the street by the police. This does not refer merely to the infiltration of the illegal drug scene by "narks" (narcotic agents). The working-class and lower middle-class sensibilities of big-city and university-town policemen are offended by the fluid, languid, unwashed, communal, antiauthoritarian, unpatriotic manifestations of the freak subculture; added to this is the intolerable thought that male freaks might be getting their share of women without looking or acting conventionally "masculine." Moreover, the freaks take for granted or even contemptuously reject "opportunities," in particular higher education, which either were denied to the typical policeman, or which he found difficult to come by. The freaks (especially if students or quasi students) may thus be regarded by the police both as "spoiled" children of a higher social stratum and as subhuman without social existence. Needless to say, the police, having been trained to be constantly alert for "suspicious-looking" persons, find the freaks to be eminently suspicious-looking. The result is routine repressive activity roughly parallel to what takes place in the black ghetto: selective and capricious enforcement of petty statutes; verbal intimidations; use of informers; harassment of automobile drivers; intimidating surveillance; conspicuous tapping of telephone lines (including selected pay phones); arbitrary searches and seizures on the street; dispersing of informal street gatherings;

clubbings; raiding of apartments and meeting places; and, increasingly, mass brutality.

Just as the black man in the streets comes to regard the policeman as the hard-core essence of whiteness, to which the conventional reality becomes simplified with its hallucinatory features seemingly stripped away; so also does the street freak define the policeman as the embodiment of "straightness" who protects the "Establishment" at every point, from the transformation of the physical environment in accordance with the dictates of the freak's shared subcultural reality, and who prevents the universal freaking-out. Freaks rapidly adopt black expressions referring to the police, such as "the Man," or, more recently, "the pigs"; in both subcultures such expressions have generalized meanings which extend to all outside authority figures and all institutionalized means of control over cultural insiders.

The black and the freak are each likely to keep one eye on the policeman's club and gun—the essence of the "system" crystallized in the form of the implements of mindless violence. But while the black man will focus the other eye on the policeman's white skin, the freak will be more preoccupied with his uniform, which is taken to symbolize repressive, hierarchical-authoritarian, routinized, self-serving, life-denying bureaucracy. Members of both subcultures become sensitive to hate stares, swaggering, and expressions of cultural bigotry and sadism; they conclude that the police are mentally ill and that they display exaggerated symptoms of mental diseases which must be pervasive in the society as a whole. The interpretations of such sicknesses naturally differ: blacks will see the effects on the "honkies' " culture of centuries of maintaining white racism; freaks will detect the consequences of the systematic institutionalized encouragement of personal violence and the "putting down" of man by man as well as the systematic suppression of sex, beauty, "life."

Black-consciousness and freak-consciousness, involving experience of "real worlds" discontinuous from the legal "real world" dictate a total rejection of the social order, either by intensifying experience of the subcultural reality within the bosom of the "community" (more a spiritual than a geographical entity), or by awaiting the Apocalypse ("Burn America down to the ground!" "Fuck the system!"), or both at once. The constant and routine cultural-political collisions with the police result in spontaneous outbursts —not necessarily of overt violence—in which the people constituting the "scene" assert their possession of the environment in question, using any means considered morally acceptable in terms of the explicit or implicit values of the subculture. The conflict over possession of the environment comes to take on some of the appearance and spirit of a youth-gang struggle over "turf." (Often the word "turf" is used explicitly, but even when the contested environment is called a "liberated area," the meaning is the same). So, while consciousness dictates the dissident's generalized antagonism to every organized institution and order of social priorities, he will finally go into action over situation-conflicts that are local and immediate: to prove that he is a man or that he exists; to be with his friends; because "they" have beaten up one of "our" women; because "they" have encroached on "our" sidewalk or park. For this he will burn down Los Angeles, Detroit, or Washington, seize a university, or assault the Democratic Party.

Bertram D. Wolfe describes the development of street action in San Francisco in 1967:

> The result of all the newspaper and television coverage was not only greater influx of hippies, but also an influx of tourists and curiosity-seekers driving automobiles down Haight Street. At times, the line of vehicles resembled a Los Angeles freeway minus five lanes during the weekend beach exodus. The hippies took offense.
>
> It was not only tourists in automobiles who were destroying their street, their center of the universe, but policemen pestered them for loitering. Why should they be pestered because of a few old ladies' complaints about the mob scene in front of Tracy's Doughnut Shop? The street was *theirs,* and to prove it, they held stand-ins, walk-ins, mill-ins, dance-ins and jam-ins. Before the major jam-in on Sunday, April 2, the Diggers tried to organize the action with a leaflet asking Hashberryites to participate in the "love feast," the name they used to get away from the newspaper oriented "ins." The leaflet instructed:
>
> "If the Man busts you, go limp! If he really wants you, let the Man carry you away like a sack of government surplus corn meal, which may even give him a hernia or heart attack!"
>
> The love generation started the happening with a march down Haight Street, headed by three young men bearing a mock barricade sign: "STREET CLOSED." Gradually, more than a thou-

sand of them gathered to sing, dance, blow soap bubbles, play flutes, and chant: "Street Closed. Street Closed." And it was—blocked traffic took care of that—until the police broke it up.[2]

This sort of street action was consistent with the joyously anti-violent cultural style of hippieism at its height, and with such slogans as "Flower Power," "Be Gentle," and "Make Love Not War." But, as my friend Evan Stark, a young activist-sociologist, pointed out to some Columbia University radicals in April 1967, "The soldier fucks *and* fights."

In traditional bourgeois culture women who put too much of the stuff on the market are considered "cheap"; a special responsibility is imposed on women to maintain the scarcity of the commodity by exacting from men a high "price" in terms of expenditure of energy in elaborate courtship rituals and expenditure of money on goods ancillary to courtship (jewelry, dinners in expensive restaurants, and so forth). It was explained that this restriction of the supply was "all that separates us from the beasts of the field." It was further held that this impulse control explained and legitimatized the hegemony of the Euro-American bourgeoisie over the "improvident" domestic lower classes—who allegedly fornicated without restraint—and later over conquered foreign peoples of darker hue as well (e.g., "the fleshpots of the East"). Given the subsequent disposition of women to increase the supply, it was probably inevitable that there should take place a system adaptation by which a harmonious balance would be preserved between overt sexuality and the repressively maintained artificial scarcity of things-in-general such that the demand continues to be greater than the available supply, and, in particular, greater than the availability of those women possessing unusual physiological features the desirability of which is reinforced by incessant propaganda.

The status of individual women continues to be in part determined by sexual selectivity, and that of individual men by sexual promiscuity; the abortion laws continue to represent a massive, scandalous, and barbarous hypocrisy; no male equivalent of "nymphomaniac" is in common speech; to refuse a "willing" woman is to violate a powerful cultural taboo; and so on; the impact, nonmeasurable, of all this upon the mutual enjoyment by men and women of sexual intercourse can only be surmised.

Aside from overt sexuality, the "straights" were confronted with exuberant contempt for organized violence as well as for the emphasis on personal violence in the conventional culture; the freaks relied on the unpredictability, sense of humor, and that capacity to disorient the enemy that is derived from expanded consciousness—often called "cosmic mind force":

> There is a definite thing—when we talk, when we use the word "power" kind of thing. It's not a sort of power in the sense that it's a vicious thing or anything. It's just the people that have a realization that they have the power. Sometimes . . . there were some people riding around [San Francisco] at night. They had just taken LSD, just enjoying the city, very beautiful ride kind of thing, you know, just really enjoying the buildings and the sidewalks and the people and all and the police car came up beside them and saw that they were, you know, like loaded and just sort of crunched them over to the curb and forced them over and the five of them got out of the car and the police were behind them and for some reason they all just ran around and didn't say anything and looked at the police, just like that, you know, that sort of look, and the police got back in the car and drove away. It's 'cause they knew they couldn't overcome that presence. It would be ridiculous for them to even talk to those people. They couldn't even communicate with them. They just—the best thing for them to do was just go away and let them alone.[3]

It was consistent with the cultural style of hippieism for the street freaks to give flowers to the police, or for hippie girls to kiss them. When arrested, the most hard-core, freaked-out specimens apparently tried to disorient "the Man" by their serenity and absolute confidence in their discontinuous reality; according to Wolfe, such tactics had their successes:

> The streets were for people, the hippies kept telling the police. And after awhile, the police began to believe it.
> Even when arrests were made, the attitude of the hippies punished the police more than jail punished the hippies. These were no beatniks scowling and skulking in an attitude of defeat. Hippies walked into jail with pride and sass. Charlie Brown wanted to be placed in solitary, the place reserved for the worst punishment. Hohn Keskulla, one of the New Communityites arrested at the Human Be-in, rejected probation and a suspended sentence because of the conditions that were attached. "Nobody's going to tell me how to live," he said. Another hippie, calling himself Ash Tray, set himself up for thirty days by refusing to answer questions on a

probation report in a straight manner; he listed his year of birth as 2000 and his occupation as Rain Dancer. When Wallace Healey, one of the original crew of the Blue Unicorn, was arrested for jumping nude into a Golden Gate Park pond, he defied a policeman to shoot him and ran away. Later, he was picked up anyway and questioned. Why had he run from the officer? "To see if he would shoot me." What was his occupation? "World Citizen." Where did he live? "In the center of the universe." Why was he bathing nude in the park against park regulations? "To talk to a friend about Jesus. It was a happening that cleansed the body and the spirit."

They could throw them into jail, but they could not change that attitude. And in the end, perhaps it was the attitude, even more than the numbers, that defeated the police.[4]

Presumably contributing to this "attitude" was the characteristic hippie notion that it is possible to throw oneself far enough into one's own subjectivity to "groove" on almost anything:

> "It doesn't really bother me to spend the night in jail or to spend time in jail here or there . . . because there are interesting things happening in there. I'm sure I wouldn't like to do time—but I'm sure if it ended up that I had to do a year—you have to get behind it no matter what it is—if you get behind it you can enjoy it—make yourself enjoy it.[5]

But a new cultural style, The Revolution, now holds sway on the streets. The hippie image has been supplanted by that of the freak-rebel who, relatively speaking, de-emphasizes—though hardly abandons—drugs and inner search, while instead emphasizing the overt struggle against the "system." The freak-rebel would agree with Jerry Rubin ("The King of the Yippies") that "Revolutionaries are good in bed." This change in images and stereotypes does not really require that there be that much change in the thoughts and routine daily activities of the average street freak; while in a crisis he is just helping out his friends, in an existential sort of way.

The new cultural style emerged from a complex and intricate interaction of developments on at least three different planes: political events (such as the "escalation" of the War in Vietnam) and social upheavals (such as the great wave of black ghetto rebellions of the summer of 1967) of national or even international importance, which glaringly demonstrated the obsolescence of the hippie political posture and order of cultural priorities (i.e., that the hippie stance was no longer "where it's at"—that it was now a species of false consciousness); routine irritations and seemingly increasing oppressiveness by police and other authorities against both the hippies and the New Left radicals, such that the hippies were becoming more overt in their hatred of the police, while the drug culture was spreading among the radicals, and the mystique of "nonviolence" was evaporating among both; and the maturation of and population changes in the various freak "scenes." It is the third level that is immediately of interest.

The black lower-class street rebel was typically born in the Northern ghetto where he operates; he is typically not a rural Southern migrant. He became "street wise" in that neighborhood, and its streets are, in an important sense, his home. But the black street "scene" is surrounded by a *black* neighborhood inhabited by hundreds, thousands, tens of thousands of black people of all ages, and including a very large percentage with steady income and employment; most of the "working age" youths on the street would take steady employment *if* it existed and *if* it were offered on culturally acceptable terms (the latter condition being increasingly more difficult to fulfill). On the other hand, the freak scene or "free community" is almost by definition a high concentration of a *youth* subculture (with outside age limits of, say, fourteen to thirty). It may be proximate to a large urban university; in this case it is an ill-defined part of a culturally diverse, apartment-dwelling youth ghetto, which also includes ordinary, "straight" undergraduate students, graduate and professional students, recent graduates and dropouts who hang around, part-time students, miscellaneous and assorted "interesting people," and pure and simple scum and lowlife. Within this youth ghetto, the freaks and quasi freaks exert a cultural and stylistic leadership out of all proportion to their numbers. It must share a slum or semislum with a culturally alien "indigenous" population, and share the streets with the indigenous youth. The local inhabitants may themselves be impoverished and radically oppressed, as is the case with the Puerto Rican and black population of New York City's Lower East Side, which is the same place as the freaks' East Village. The following is an excerpt from the San Francisco *Oracle,* in which a hippie ideologist explains the development of the freak ghetto in

San Francisco's Haight-Ashbury district as a mass flight from compulsive consumption and bureaucratic routines:

The street scene has become an entrance into a phenomenon to which we have all been invited. The word has been passed throughout the country, compliments of the above ground media, that there is a scene going down on Haight St. The most receptive to the call are from middle class urbia. They leave jobs, armies and schools to turn their lives and psyches inside out, all looking for some material to build a life with. All of us started to realize, even in 17 or 20 short years, that the game of life played in school and the supermarket U. leads only to styrofoam coffins and oblivous servitude. Most of us have been on the threshold of jumping into the accepted swim, but stop and ask for time, having already seen enough instinctively, if not intellectually. Few have talents or skills developed enough for personal satisfaction or for the marketplace; all are well trained toward indiscriminate consumption. Yet the feeling persists—there must be something greater than this!

The street becomes where it's at. It is easy to get laid there, cop dope, find a friend or a mate. Books and ideas, acid and pot, the nearby park, or a pad full of music form a surreal montage of the constant weekend.

How else in America today can the Protestant Ethic be wrung out? To learn the reality of fantasy and the fantasy of reality? It is a process of steady deculturalization, to clear your head of the Mustang Pledge and the nonsense of a chicken in every Dodge Rebellion. Running in opposite directions of childhood conditioning, looking for perspective by playing roles, wearing costumes and dropping acid. LSD becomes a sacrificial deconditioner expanding consciousness, allowing each person to actually experience the logic of self-discovery. . . . The street scene and its extensions into the art and living patterns that are being developed is in large part due to what is first envisioned and then consciously applied through the use of LSD and . . . almost inevitably removes a person from the transitory superficial machinations of western society . . . a society which consciously strives to prevent this sort of looking around.

It takes time and experience to reintegrate these new forms of knowledge and personality into a comfortable living pattern. In the meantime some people use the limbo of street life and drop practically every material possession to live solely by their wits. They sleep in parks, on doorsteps when the commune is full, live at night and rest by day. Scrounge food, shoot meth, hustle college kids coming to gawk and get laid, just as their fathers when nigger wasn't spelled negro. Work as a last resort but better to play or hitch to Big Sur. Bohemia is no longer refuge for a few, the third V.P.'s daughter wants in, too. Hepatitis, hunger, crabs and clap, freak out and then on to the next scene. Frantic searching, then slow growth, learn to let go, live only on what you need. How long does it take to dig where you're at and catch on to the scene? There is no one to tell you now, but only file cabinets can lie.

The street can be a classroom, a zoo, a stage, an asphalt padded cell, a whorehouse, a folksong or the traverse of Scorpio. Fashions develop for brown rice and the I Ching, for farms and Indians, '47 panel trucks, beads and books. Most of us have gone through something like it, possibly they are at first only bourgeois allusions of freedom, in attempting to find what is real for ourselves and what is comfortable. The street is there and some must run its course, called doing their thing, going through changes. Other less mangled are able to deculturalize or find themselves easier, but the educational conformist pressures stack higher against them. It can be done anywhere but our society tends to produce exaggerations of itself and only extremity seems to break through its accompanying neurosis. Thus the phenomenon of street life, a clearing house spontaneously formed to break the conditioning of the perpetual motion machine. People running away from disaster without a place to go, only an idea of where it might be found. (Richard Honigman, "Flower From The Street," San Franciso *Oracle,* August 1967).

A possible factor in the initial plausibility of the hippie stance with respect to overt struggle, i.e., refraining from it, may have been a certain complacency about the dangers of the street carried over from the secure, routine daily life in the middle-class lifestyles being abandoned. In 1966 and early 1967 there was tremendous expansion of the hippie, drug-culture population; most of the people involved were new converts, with LSD only recently generally available, while marijuana use had been associated primarily with the black lower class until 1961 or 1962, and spread from small coteries of students and "beatniks." Drug users and protohippies of my acquaintance in Syracuse in early 1967 talked incessantly about the police, encounters with the police, outwitting the police, with special emphasis on the analysis of the personality, habits, and mannerisms of the police sergeant in charge of the narcotics squad. A certain romantic thrill was combined with feelings of impotence and of being treated like hunted animals. Obsessive-compulsive precautions often alternated with what proved to be catastrophic carelessness. Then came the busts, the continual presence of informers among one's brothers, the personal experience of police brutality, so that by the end of 1968 not even the most apolitical Syracuse street freak could possibly bring himself to write that the police had his "respect"; far too many people had been arrested for that. As for the notion that the police are "just doing their job," that, in the politicized climate of 1968, appeared as a manifestation of the fundamental moral issue in society. It has become a matter of overt folk ideology that nobody should "just do his job" if he thereby becomes the instrumentality of a bureaucratic superior who perpetrates evil by infringing on the freedom of others to "do their own thing." Such infringement is automatically classified as "fascism."

The other problem faced on the streets, especially in places like the East Village-Lower East Side in New York City, was that of harassment by lower-class and working-class youths, the latter including motorcycle gangs. The local youth on the Lower East Side seem to have regarded the hippies as a species of invading middle-class perverts; with some justification, they did not take seriously the hippies' efforts to repudiate their middle-class origins and their social existence, or to assert the identity of the police as the common enemy. Moreover, the hippies had women without knowing how to fight; this, in the slums, is considered a species of grave immorality. The freaks of the Lower East Side had to become "street wise" with respect to both the police and the local youths, or go under and move out. The problem was partially solved from the other direction when the Puerto Rican youths of the neighborhood rioted, for entirely their own reasons, as derived from their own class and racial oppression, in mid-July 1968.

Thus, at a time of generally intensifying political and social crisis, the freak population was constantly changing. Some were migrating from one city to another; others were becoming hardened in the defense of their life-style on the streets; others returned to some semblance of the middle-class lives whence they came; still others were arriving on the street having freaked out directly into the revolution; and there were now a considerable number of student radicals still in school. These changes, combined with continual forced experiencing of the street as a dangerous and brutal turf, capped by several instances of police attacks upon street freaks for apparently no reason other than that they were hanging out on the street (see, for example, the attack described by Jerry Densch in "Haight Street Blues," *The Movement,* September 1967) led to the emergence of the freak-rebel, with his logic of "Democracy Is in the Streets," "The Streets Belong to the People," "We Are the People." The freak-rebel does not give the police any flowers but instead chants, "Pig! Pig! Pig! Oink! Oink! Oink!" or maybe throws a Molotov cocktail.

CHAPTER 10

The Freak-Rebel

In the age of industrialization, the dissident builds organizations. In the age of mature industrialization and subjectivist ideologies, the dissident becomes a symbolic center—a lightning rod of symbolic energy.

As indicated earlier, the nineteenth- and early twentieth-century industrialization of Western-Central Europe and the United States brought into existence a new hierarchical class society (which partly merged with and partly replaced the older class structure) in which the location and distribution of political power were thought (mistakenly or not) to be readily identifiable even by its enemies and victims who formulated their own theories of the nature, origins, and legitimacy of that power. With political, social, and economic causality open to rational study and prediction on the basis of the data available to the "public," it was concluded that the power relations in the social order could be shifted by building centralized and disciplined mass organizations. The *rationality* of this was that bureaucracy conferred upon the dissidents the same advantages it conferred upon their enemies: efficiency, rationalization of action, effective concentration of human and material resources upon a single point or objective, the ability to coordinate far-flung operations, the ability to formulate long-term plans, goals, and priorities, the ability to secure continuity of finances and other necessities of maintaining a corporate existence (e.g., strike funds, legal defense, lobbyists, propaganda activities) beyond the cooling of momentary animosities and enthusiasms of conflict—for potential use at a later date. The rationality derived, too, from the situation, characteristic of all societies until very recently, in which a generalized scarcity prevailed which necessitated considerable social discipline and repression; dissidents of the lower classes were necessarily preoccupied with the division of the economic surplus, rather than with the unrestricted development of the self.

But the affluent society now coincides with the overwhelming superiority of state and corporate bureaucracies over organizations thrown up by social movements; superiority in terms of ability to plan and manipulate; esoteric knowledge; communications, data storage, and other relevant advanced technologies; propaganda—tending to be coextensive with the entire mass culture; intelligence gathering and the ability to co-opt, bribe, infiltrate, and engage in surveillance, espionage, planned disruption, and other covert and clandestine activities; and, of course, in the preponderance of the means of violence potentially available. I have touched on all of this before.

An entirely new political logic therefore emerges, in which "politics" tends to disappear as a discrete and readily identifiable category of human behavior segmented out of the total context of culture and personality. Simultaneously, the freak-radical does not let his energies get absorbed in "building an organization" or "attacking issues." Instead, he joins with others in small groups based on friendship, or the sharing of common or parallel experiences. These groups also serve as nuclei for political activity, but their reason for being is personal, not political (insofar as one can make such a distinction). In the freak subculture, the distinction between "public" and "private" has collapsed; the "private" forms the basis of the "public" activity, and overt politics can become an overlay upon friendship and "informal" associations.

These nonorganizations are the structural counterpart of the subjectivist ideology. As I hope I have already made clear, the need for subjectivist ideologies arises in the first place because objective social reality is so complicated, changes so swiftly, and is disguised by so many complex and many-layered hallucinations, delusions, and counterdelusions (which are, of course, ultimately perpetuated by an objective, material, and quite real set of institutions, structures, class hierarchies, and unequal distributions of power) that a potential dissident who relies on his personal experiences, feelings, dreams, and even drug fantasies, can hardly come up with worse hallucinations than he could find in the political propaganda of "mainstream" institutions and "legitimate agencies for change"—assuming that the roots of his discontent correspond to an objectively real historical situation. Often, as I think I have shown, he can do very much better.

Just as the multitude of legal drugs (tranquilizers, alcohol, etc.) serves mainly to depress the individual's subjective awareness, the illegal hallucinogens associated with the freak subculture—marijuana and LSD—throw the user more deeply into the reality of everyday life, to the point where an absolute contradiction is established in consciousness between immediate experience and what appear to be distortions of experience implanted by institutional necessities, i.e., the entire belief-concept-image-metaphor-feeling structure used for the interpretation of social reality. One distinguishes between what appears to be the substance of particular situations and "words they made up," while bureaucratic euphemisms (e.g., "counterproductive" for "worse than useless") and subterfuges, parliamentary ritual, polite pretense, official titles, manners, "good breeding," language disinfected for "public" purposes, work routines and time schedules, courtship rituals, lecture formats, appear as so much "bullshit," nothing more. LSD, in particular, has effects upon individual consciousness analogous to that of electronic media upon culture—this having been noted publicly by both Timothy Leary (the LSD theorist) and Marshall McLuhan (the media theorist; "our electronic brother," as Leary called him)—apparently by partial suppression of culturally standardized personality mechanisms which restrict the flow of sensory data and association-fragments into awareness, and which thus permit the relatively uncluttered operation of culturally implanted "logical" processes. The consequent multiplication and speeding up of the flow of information into awareness vastly increases the probability of the forced juxtaposition of irreconcilable elements; when this happens, the tripper experiences the Absurd and collapses into giggling fits, finding momentary relief by means of concentration upon sensory stimuli (such as music or bright colors), perhaps to the point of pain. Rigid conceptual structures are undermined and mangled, multiple levels of causality are perceived in operation simultaneously, emotions are wrenched loose from their conceptual moorings (the tripper then goes on a wild emotional roller coaster ride called "going through the changes"; he can cry and giggle simultaneously, realize he is doing it, and be both horrified and amused at himself), elaborate conceptual structures of delightful senselessness form and dissolve ceaselessly, infinite regress-paradoxes rage out of control, and, what is most relevant here, the ideologies, symbols, and conventional beliefs legitimating all hierarchal authorities and organized institutions whatsoever are reduced to ludicrous nonsense, combined with fearful realizations of the ultimately violent basis of their power. ("There are no kings inside the Gates of Eden.") Only the demands of the self appear real; the demands of institutions appear as "unreal" impositions.

The drug culture thus functions among middle-class youths to reinforce an already existing sense of undue restriction by superfluous social discipline. It undermines the legitimacy and image of quasi permanence attached to the dominant middle-class life-styles —and by extension undermines the legitimacy of the institutions which sustain those life-styles; stimulates personality changes that decrease the inclination to "function" in the standard types of institutional contexts; and encourage behavioral experimentation which has its logical conclusion in the street freak's life-style, including the distinctive physical appearance which he prizes as his equivalent of the black man's skin. Efforts to suppress the drug culture provide an egregious example of the intersection of conventional hallucination and irrational authoritarianism which is readily used as a model for the war in Vietnam, racism, or conventional sexual attitudes, and synthesized into a world view; the existence of a totalistic antiauthoritarian ideology—however inane its manifestations may appear—associated with the drug culture reassures a discontented individual (say, a college freshman living away from his family for an extended period for the first time in his life) that his feelings are not mere personal neurosis. Perhaps most important, the drug experiences provide what appear to be free and uncontrolled self-creation, the generalized expression of which is called one's Thing—and since one's Thing is an expression of the "real" self, it should, in principle, be done all the time. The subjective experience of self-creation, free of institutional constraints, is called "being" (a term picked up from the Existentialists and existential psychologists).

The drug culture, which spans everything from the totally and permanently freaked-out acid-head to the teen-ager smoking his first joint, is thus an essential element of a radical subculture that (together with rock music, which disorients the listener or dancer with throbbing rhythms or deliberately outlandish noises, and other cultural manifestations) is furthermore accessible to masses of people without any intellectual inclinations or abilities. (Something not true of the New Left-SDS "analysis"—though this is often reduced to the level of clichés plus adrenalin, and much of SDS is thoroughly stoned.) Associated, in its more intense manifestations, with an ideology of totalistic and apocalyptic rejection of "the system," it reduces the inclination of individuals to function as components of a social system. To the extent that the social order is indeed a system—as well as a hierarchical class society—anything that prevents individuals or institutions from functioning must be considered (at least to some extent) as a valid, logical, and rational political response.

In the same way, the development of what I shall call "affinity groups"—nonstructured political nuclei—is a valid structural response. In the ideal-typical case, the political nucleus is formed by a small group of very close friends who feel forced into certain courses of action by the stituational necessities of environments crucial to the life-style of the subculture. The Black Panther Party was founded in October 1966 by Huey P. Newton (Minister of Defense) and Bobby Seale (Chairman). According to Eldridge Cleaver (Minister of Information): "Bobby has known Huey Newton for approximately eight years, dating back to their days at Merritt College in Oakland." Seale, Newton, and others who constituted the original inner circle were of lower-class origins ("righteous boys off the block," as Bobby Seale puts it), and had become a tightly knit clique at Merritt College, partly as a result of friction with "jive" cultural-nationalist students of middle-class origin. They had first formed the Soul Students Advisory Council. According to Bobby Seale's account:

> Me and Huey decided we was going to try and make the thing work. A college campus group, to develop it, and to help develop leadership, to go to the black community and serve the black community in a revolutionary fashion.

This, at first, meant endless agitation on the streets, including expounding the ideas of Frantz Fanon. These activities attracted the attention of the tough Oakland police; the Black Panther Party, together with the practice of the open display of guns on the street —central to the party's myth and style—developed out of the need to counterintimidate the police.

The Diggers (founded in September 1966), the hippie "invisible government" and service organization in Haight-Ashbury (and later in New York and Chicago), followed the same pattern. And the freak-rebels (who now call themselves "street people") of the Lower East Side-East Village generated the Up Against the Wall / Motherfuckers in similar fashion. During the New York City Department of Sanitation strike of February 1968, an incident occurred in which street freaks threw garbage at the police. The Motherfuckers were inspired to develop their Thing, a semispontaneous street riot called the "henry": the Motherfuckers would pass the word, "Big henry tonight," and hundreds of street freaks would gather on the streets, disrupting traffic, setting trash cans afire, harassing police in side streets, and rendezvousing in Washington Square Park to find shelter from the police among the hordes of tourists.

In late 1968, the freak population of the same neighborhood generated another entity called "Lowereast Side Defense" (LSD) which, distinguished by red headbands, engaged in countersurveillance of the police, under the slogan, "Defend our streets!"

Although most freaks are white middle-class youths, spontaneous dissidence by young people in the white working class has also erupted: "rank-and-file-ism" in the trade unions, the increase in "wildcat" work stoppages in 1967–1968, and a simultaneous, increasing reluctance to ratify contracts negotiated by entrenched trade-union bureaucrats. (When the Utility Workers struck Consolidated Edison in December 1968 after rejecting the contract originally negotiated by their union, a group of younger workers celebrated by joyously waving the "underground" V-sign, as shown in a photograph in the *Guardian* for December 14, 1968.) Spontaneous antiauthoritarian dissidence among young white workers —like that of young black workers in the Dodge Revolutionary Union Movement of Hamtramck, Michigan—is likely to be directed against both union and employer bureaucracies; and it will be a carry-over into the work situation of a subculture developed outside the plant. White lower-class and working-class youths, like black lower-class youths, and unlike white middle-class youths, grow up on central-city streets, where they hang out, get into fights, and often face what look like bleak and boring lives without either the class privileges of education or the exciting mystique of "revolution." They prize the ability to fight; working-class toughs have been known to call profusely bearded freaks "girl" on suspicion that the latter have no taste for fighting. They form street gangs: the "outlaw" motorcycle gangs such as the Hell's Angels of California, the Headhunters of Chicago, and the Outcasts of Syracuse, none of whom have any love for the authorities. Hell's Angels attacked peace marchers in Oakland in 1966, but fought alongside street freaks in Berkeley in June 1968, as the Headhunters did in Chicago in August, and as the Outcasts almost did during a hot night in Syracuse in September (the event did not get past the stage of mutual glowering between police and street people).

As subjectivist consciousness develops, we would expect to find "politics" becoming more and more indistinguishable from the general activities of "informal"-friendship cliques and networks; individuals in these networks may also be members of formal organizations, but they act in solidarity with their friends, not in solidarity with their organizations. Solidarity in a community (geographically bound) or a "scene" (in principle, independent of geography), as well as the transmission and intensification of a subculture, depends upon informal, diffuse, and prolonged interaction among individuals. This basis of solidarity comes to be accepted as the normative ideal: only "the streets," i.e., unstructured social spaces, are real. The black lower-class youths, who have grown up on the streets, have been told that the reality of everyday life is a fake universe, the product of failure and racial inferiority; they therefore turn all the definitions around and insist that the rest of society is a fraud and a system of genocidal racist oppression. White middle-class youths, who have grown up indoors in a series of rectangular boxlike environments, come to suspect that the reality of everyday life is a fake universe; and an indicative minority of them also turns all the definitions around and insists that "bourgeois reality" must be judged and attacked from the standpoint of "the streets."

The dissident desires not a reorganization of institutions, so much as a condition of generalized withdrawal of social and institutional constraints ("Everything"), to permit free, ongoing self-creation ("Anything"). But to communicate with the cultural-political enemy, he is required to deal separately with each one of the latter's institutional structures impinging on his life and present a list of "demands" to it. This not only forces him into stable, structured relationships with the enemy, but does so on the grounds of the enemy's greatest advantage—where the apparatus of negotiation and conflict-resolution is brought into play. He ultimately senses that his only restraint over the cultural-political enemy is the latter's understanding that he can freak out at any time without giving off any warning signals even to himself. William H. Grier and Price M. Cobbs, two black psychiatrists, tell of conscious awareness in the ghettos regarding the advantages conferred by the propensity to freak out beyond the control of standard negotiating channels:

> During recent riots there was a wry saying in the ghetto. "Chuck can't tell where it's going to hit next because we don't know ourselves." And it was a fact. The most baffling aspect to rioting in Newark, Detroit, and Watts was the complete spontaneity of the violence. Authorities turned to "responsible" Negro leaders to calm the black rebels and the Negro leaders did not know where to start. They were confronted with a leaderless mob which needed no leader. Every man was a leader—they were of one mind.[1]

The further conclusion to be drawn from this is that political action, in such indicative minorities as black-ghetto, street-youth scenes and street-freak radical scenes, should be the spontaneous, freaked out, mutually supportive action of intensely and diffusely interacting friendship groups who encounter each other and hang out in the streets and in street-related environments. And this is what actually happens: Black Nationalist groups, as already noted, are often street gangs with intensified cultural-political consciousness; the intensified consciousness may develop in the wake of black-ghetto riots or rebellions—or it may have preceded them. In the rebellions themselves, of course, it was the street-gang youths who everywhere played the leading role, whether in the great out-bursts (Watts, Newark, Detroit) or in minor spasms. Among white freaks, such groups may be known alternatively as "gangs," "affinity groups," "tribes," "families," or "communes." [2] (French versions of the "affinity group" played crucial roles in their Revolution of May 1968.) [3] Or Jerry Densch's observations:

> If anything is happening [in Haight-Ashbury], it is in the communes and "families," off the street.
> People may not be talking about "affinity groups" as centers of resistance, like they are in Berkeley, but the groups are there, and the potential for them to act in a politically meaningful way is certainly there too.
> Small groups of people, often living under the same roof, in which there is a feeling of trust and brotherhood not found on the street, may soon become the source of action in the Haight.[4]

An important function of these political nuclei—the affinity groups—is the living out of the subcultural conception of total freedom—as interpreted by the cultural insiders in their prevailing level of consciousness, and for as long as it can be gotten away with. The leader of the black-dissident nucleus must provide a model of the defiant throwing-off of white restraints which accompanies the free development and expression of a black self; he communicates a poetic, beautiful, and dramatic black experience. The white-youth dissident leader similarly demonstrates his complete emancipation from conventional white middle-class culture while communicating an impression of his "inner beauty." Both movements have their saints, prophets, seers, holy men, rebels who live for the moment and for the sheer joy of the struggle, mystics, and men who went down fighting or were otherwise martyred for living out the subcultural ideal to its fullest measure. The leader, then, is not so much a politician as a *metaphor*.

The hero is a hero not so much because of any specific heroic deeds he may have performed, but because he dares to live out his life-style to the fullest extent, conveying the impression that he is "free," i.e., guided solely by the dictates of his own subjectivity, and daring to persistently invade and injure the environments of the cultural-political enemy despite all the obviously repressive sanctions at the enemy's command. He abandons all restraints ("lets it all hang out," "kicks out all the jams," is "together" and "does his own thing"), and gives free expression to the life energies which, other members of the subculture feel, must be kept bottled up because of the practical necessities and expediencies of everyday life; yet he also appears to be "ready to die." In doing all this, the hero necessarily assaults the distinction between "public" and "private": dissidents experience "public" environments as not only booby-trapped with artificial constraints on the fluidity of social interaction and individual behavior, but also as under the forcible control of the white or "straight" cultural-political enemy.[5]

The white middle-class youth movement tends to have little tolerance for authoritarianism within itself; its leaders attack the principle of the concentration of power in the hands of leaders (even while, as often happens, they are trying to increase their power at the time). One of the worst insults in the New Left lexicon is "manipulative elitism." New Leftists such as Tom Hayden and Mark Rudd have complained (validly) that they have been artificially built up as symbols by the mass media. Freak-radicals go even farther: Yippie leaders, who have called themselves "non-leaders" and "energy sources," have come up with such slogans as "Every man his own revolution!"

Many veteran student activists experience guilt, anxiety, or fear when confronted with the necessity for the repressive use of authority; and freak anarchism has captured the imagination of a large part of the "base." It remains almost impossible to conduct an SDS meeting at any level—chapter, regional, or national—without a good deal of random discussion, or even chaos and disorder. Veteran activists become acutely conscious of the need to avoid the fetishism of structure for its own sake; a young woman on the National Office staff wrote as follows to campus organizers on the need for informal interaction in building up regional structures:

> I work on the basis of the educational conference because I know that business meetings tend to turn people off, leading to apathy rather than involvement. The region must serve some vital function in its members, and tho the ed. conf. is not the only one, it's the only one I've been able to think of that has the pos-

sibility of sustaining itself. I'd like to hear other ideas on how to make our infra-structure real and vital, so that we can radically change the nature of organizational bureaucracies. It's important, I think, to develop these middle-level structures, since the country is so large leading to the very large lack of contact between chapter members and the national. Also, since we are trying to create a society in which people can enter into the decision-making process as whole people, we need to search out political and administrative forms that more nearly involve the whole person. Any ideas on how? [6]

"Radicalization," in SDS jargon, refers not to education in a radical doctrine, or membership in a radical organization, but to a thorough emotional transformation affecting the individual's entire life. As Gregory Calvert put it while speaking as National Secretary of SDS:

> Radical or revolutionary consciousness . . . is the discovery of oneself as one of the oppressed who must unite to transform the objective conditions of their existence in order to resolve the contradiction between potentiality and actuality. . . .
> When we have talked about the "new radicalism," about the "freedom movement," with a passionate conviction, we have been talking about a movement which involves us, you and me, in a gut-level encounter with, disengagement from, and struggle against the America which keeps us in bondage. [7]

I will suggest that the reason these children of the white middle class—and the children of the black lower class as well—are not forced to respond to the "necessity" of adopting the virtue of "efficiency," "practicality," "orderly and businesslike procedure," and "concrete step-by-step progress toward an attainable goal," etc., and thereby be induced to develop organizational forms more of the "Old Left" type, is that they are—perhaps more unconsciously than consciously—responding to the same political universe that was taken as given by the large conglomerate corporation which submitted a proposal to the federal government for funding, in which it was maintained that the problems of a certain black ghetto could be solved by treating the city in question as a "system" with 135 "subsystems"—the "technotronic" world (to use the word coined by the political scientist Dr. Zbigniew Brzezinski of Columbia) of advanced technology and complexly inter-related institutions in which the sophisticated decision-maker or policy-planner operates.

Consider the society solely as a social *system* (while forgetting for the moment about a hierarchy of mutually antagonistic *classes*). If you have decided that you are somehow a "revolutionary," you cannot be sure, first of all, whether your adoption or even this role is not itself "functional" for the system as a whole. You are, in any case, part of the system to the extent that you stimulate the development of the economic system by spending money on consumer goods. There is, in this limiting case, no ruling class to overthrow, only a structurally differentiated subsystem with planning, total-system goal formulating, total-system and intra-system boundary maintenance, resource allocation, and other functions. It would be further indicated that there is no sense in your building a structure which is intended to seize control of and drastically modify a single institutional subsystem, since the pattern-maintenance processes of the total system will then come into play; the functional requirements of the subsystem that falls under your control have been adapted to inputs from and outputs to other subsystems, and these will operate to compel you to restore something very much like the original arrangement. It also makes no sense for you to assemble, over an extended period of time, a structure intended to be dysfunctional to the total system, since the latter will either liquidate your structure while leaving itself plenty of margin for its own safety—or it will permit your structure to accommodate and become an accepted part of the larger system. So you encourage people spontaneously to dissolve parts of the system into a condition of social fluidity, chaos, and disorder; for a brief period, before the pattern is restored, they will have acted out an antireality hitherto existing only in fantasy wishes; you will perhaps also have set off secondary dissolutions elsewhere. There is always the chance that a chain of dissolutions will be set off which cannot be contained and which will culminate in the entire social system being unraveled into chaos (though this can never be counted upon in any given instance).

Nobody consciously reasons along these lines, and certainly not in these terms. It is, however, possible to reconstruct the emerging political logic from cultural-ideological manifestations and mass behavior during crises. First, look at the two sides in any potential crisis: on the one side will be bureaucratic organizations and their officials, accustomed to negotiating with other organized entities, or otherwise dealing arbitrarily with isolated individuals. On the other side are the substantially unarmed dissidents, who are unorganized but who share a common subculture marked by total-istic-antiauthoritarian impulses which can be represented in the form of a slogan, thus:

> i want
> something
> NOW!
> but i don't
> know what
> it is [8]

Recent university uprisings display the workings out of such a confrontation. The "student"—if he so identifies himself—ration-alizes his presence at college in terms of "getting an education" qualifying him for a "career"—and his family has presumably "invested" a lot of money in this. He is thus time-bound, and locked into one of the most powerful social myths of the society (and of the middle classes in particular). He may sense that he is being "channeled" by the "system" into a way of life he despises, fraught with irrational social discipline; he may sense that the university is—despite its bland exteriors and dignified manners—"part of the system" and implicated in monstrous evils; but he will, even if a "student radical," retain his acceptance of the "education-career" complex under all but the most extreme situations—for "public" purposes, at least—and will resent efforts to convert the university into political turf with the accompanying interference with the tight schedule of classes, papers, examinations. At most he will demand "student power" and a "restructured university"—by which, at bottom, he is reconciling his visceral hatred of the pre-vailing level and modes of social discipline throughout the social order, with his equally visceral fear of being denied the material and status rewards of that social order, should it happen to sur-vive. When he is truly freaked out, on the other hand, he simul-taneously repudiates the "careers" of the conventional future ("doing the Man's dirty work") along with the concept of "educa-tion" in the conventional present:

> . . . us refusing to buy their line, or be what they need us to be. Dancing in their corridors, screaming at their speeches, telling 'em we're hip to their lies.[9]

Once in this state of consciousness, his principal objective at the university becomes the complete smashing of its existing institutional relationships (the "critical university") as a step in the precipitation of the total Apocalypse and social dissolution; for only the total freak-out of everything can make possible the triumph of the new culture and its values.

Political nuclei have broadened the boundaries of "political relevance" immensely, revealing the political significance of hair, music, loitering, speech patterns, food, and, in fact, everything. "Politics" is, after all, a word in people's heads associated in the conventional culture with meanings having restrictive implications as to its content; in the new movements, the rebellion against the repressed existence of everyday life tends to press against these restrictions and burst through them. As Abbie Hoffman summarized repressed existence: "ABOLISH PAY TOILETS, MAN!" he shouted, causing heads to turn in the restaurant. "That's the goal of the revolution—eternal life and free toilets." (*Newsweek,* October 14, 1968.)

The friction between New Leftists and freak-radicals over "political relevance" is an expression of the Reality Gap and is at bottom a conflict between the political strategy of building an organization and the political logic of intensifying a subculture. If you think of yourself as belonging to an organization, you gain in tightly focused militancy and short-term discipline and cohesiveness; but you lose your generalized sense of the distinctiveness of your way of life and your overriding values, with the result that your struggle can degenerate into a series of mindless—but highly intellectualized—conflicts with the authorities. If you think of yourself as intensifying a subculture, you may lose the advantages —in the short run—that only organization can confer (money, the support of disciplined numbers, a coherent and detailed picture of the course of events outside your immediate experience, the ability to influence local authorities to your advantage, but you qualitatively improve your sense of who you are and where you are going, as well as your ability to respond culturally to new changes in the environment; you can also develop a kind of total solidarity which is impossible for any organization to sustain where the antiauthoritarian and antiascetic pressures are so strong. It is only the self-interest of freak consciousness (the attainment of a generalized condition of social fluidity in which the free and unfettered ongoing creation by the individual of his own self is allowed to "happen") that can motivate, over an extended period, a social movement which can become a serious political threat to the existing order.

If understood in terms of a broader analysis, therefore, this complex of subcultural globules, friendship groups, and freak-outs appears as a remarkable adaptation to the repressive potentialities of the state in advanced industrial society: the early months of the Nazi regime in Germany (i.e., by comparison with what came later, the relatively chaotic months) demonstrated conclusively that a sufficiently determined and moderately armed state could crush disciplined and elaborately organized mass parties and trade unions, with millions of members, like so many insects. World War II similarly demonstrated the ineffectuality of clandestine organizations even against the occupation regime of a foreign power: the Communists in industrialized France were capable only of harassment and sabotage against the Nazi occupiers, while their comrades in "primitive" peasant Yugoslavia were militarily able to defeat the Nazis. When presented with extreme threat, the "organizer" or "cadre" always does what is "realistically" necessary to preserve the structure or to permit subsequent reconstruction of the structure—and he always loses.

The political logic of the new movements, whether or not it is consciously understood, demands that there be no reliance on structures, which can always be smashed or manipulated, and which must be *assumed* to be infiltrated. There can be no reliance on the preservation of secrets and informational security, given infiltration, surveillance, and ultraminiaturized solid-state electronic "bugging" devices that will ultimately render torture technologically obsolete and unnecessary. There can be no reliance on plans since they will be elaborately counterplanned against. There can be no reliance on obedience to orders issued by leaders, since these leaders are potential hostages of the state. Everything must be bent toward making the dissidents as unpredictable to the computerized state as possible.

"Realism" tells us that "in unity there is strength," and "united we stand, divided we fall." In the new movements, this is no longer necessarily true. It has been argued, for example, that if the black and white movements had combined against the war in

Vietnam, opposition to that war might have been more effective. Yet the inability adequately to define political effectiveness in such situations is precisely one of the major factors conducive to the emergence of subjectivist consciousness and the new political logic in the first place. The meaning of the act to the actor comes to have priority over its meaning to the authorities. The political nucleus, increasingly a metaphor, rather than an entity engaged in "politics," comes—knowingly or otherwise—less and less to seek political effectiveness, and more and more to intensify the subculture and with it a perspective on the nature of the enemy, the nature of repressed existence, and the nature of the group identity which tends to render cultural-political consciousness utterly discontinuous from that of all cultural outsiders, including other dissident cultures. White middle-class youths, new to the experience of "police brutality," must be free to indulge their obsession with it (to the point where it almost appears they think it has been invented for their benefit). Black youths must be free to indulge their suspicions of all whites as potential exploiters and manipulators (including those whites who profess their violent opposition to "racism"). A long list of such contradictions can easily be compiled. The collaboration of both in a single structure would require a dilution of the subcultures and hence a dilution and blunting of the emotional impetus motivating each. And the focus on any specific "issue" implies the acceptance of the assumption that repressed existence is compartmentalized rather than unified; this further implies the limiting and channeling of energies back into the universe of discourse and the political logic of the conventional reality.

The new social and political forms based on the fluidity principle (scenes and street gangs–affinity groups) constitute the new society growing within the womb of the old.

The Motherfuckers, an SDS chapter, after the Democratic Convention confrontation, projected the emergence of a new class. At the core of this class are those who live permanently "outside" the social order (i.e., who do not "function" in the "system" in that they are without stable employment), having been either excluded from the "job market"—and bureaucratically routinized life in general—for reasons of poverty and racism, or having "dropped out" for reasons of cultural disgust and political disaffection. Their life-styles are fluid and institutionally unregulated; they have been denied social existence or have repudiated it; they must engage in illegal activities in order to survive; they must engage in violent conflict with the authorities to ensure the integrity of their life-styles and the security of their "communities"; and they must be young in order to be aggressive and capable combatants. This class is therefore a "social destructure." Recruited from all classes in the social structure, it exists in a state of dynamic chaos, in continually violent conflict with orderly and structured society.

Just as Marx recognized the achievement of the bourgeoisie in laying the technological foundation for the liberation of the rural masses of Europe from "the idiocy of rural life," so we must recognize the achievement of the "technostructure" in laying the technological foundation for the liberation of the masses from the idiocy of industrial life.

Just as nineteenth-century liberalism and, later, nineteenth-century socialism came to include the assumption that a human being is too precious to be wasted on anything so stupid as agriculture, so does late twentieth-century anarchism (for want of a better word) viscerally assume that a human being is too precious to be wasted on anything so stupid as industrial production.

In an agricultural society, the primary obligation of the individual was to be somehow related to the process of the production of food, either as landlord or as peasant. With industrialization, the primary obligation of the individual then became to be somehow related to the process of the manufacture of industrial goods, either as owner-manager or as proletarian. To this was later added the obligation to consume in accordance with new needs devised and inculcated at the behest of corporate industrial planners, so that the consumer-goods sector of the economy may continue to grow at the required pace. To this was finally added the ultimate perversion of nationalism—to sustain a sufficiently intense level of antagonism toward selected foreign powers such that a sufficient amount of advanced new technology continues to be fed into the system despite the risk of global annihilation.

In the postindustrial society, the next stage, the individual will not owe anything to anybody or anything for any reason whatsoever. Fluidity will be the governing principle of social existence: people may work extremely hard because they are into their Thing; or they may hang around doing nothing; neither will be prized over the other. People will cease to have careers, but will have "bags" that they are into. People will not be "hired" for "jobs" but will work together with their friends. The concepts of "education" and "labor" as compartmentalized aspects of life will vanish. Stable cultures and stable identities will not exist. Activity will be its own reward and will be the primary reward to be considered in the differential distribution of rewards in society. Government will emerge as needed and disappear when the need passes—or risk being torn limb from limb, this being universally and enthusiastically acclaimed. It will be unheard of, even for medical purposes, for anyone but the individual himself to keep and store any kind of data or information on himself. The primary obligation will, and in fact necessarily must, become the continuing creation of the self. Such is the logical end result of the strategic scarcity of knowledge.

Last Thoughts on Freak Culture

Between 1969 and 1971 the social movements of the sixties seemed to have evaporated. Insurgencies of blacks and freaks subsided and fragmented; though lower-class ethnic-subculture-based movements continue to intensify among Chicanos, Puerto Ricans, and American Indians; and, in the middle class, the sexual-politics movements of women and homosexuals may supply most of the excitement to be expected from the seventies. The new decade is thus far shaping up as a more technologically advanced and sexually libertine version of the fifties, complete with the reappearance on television screens of Lawrence Welk, Richard Nixon, and Jackie Gleason. It is a time of consciousness contraction; the decade's first big fad was, interestingly enough, Nostalgia.

To summarize briefly the last few phases of freak culture:

The New New Left (October 1967–June 1969), following months of growing cultural and intellectual sterility and inane factionalism, liquidated itself in the summer of 1969, if not earlier; the symbolic event was the SDS convention in Chicago in June, at which the organization split into factions and then vanished like the morning dew. The "leaders" of the (capital M) "Movement"—of whatever faction—had become convinced of the necessity for a "serious" revolutionary movement, by which was meant preoccupation with discipline, sacrifice, strategy and tactics, Marxist erudition, and other features of Socialism (that obsolete political subculture dating from the age of industrialization and no longer viable in postscarcity conditions).

As I have endeavored to explain, the very existence of a social movement among white middle-class youth was caused by the end of material scarcity; this change in objective social conditions brought about a change in social character, while institutions remained comparatively stable. One might say that the "pleasure principle" was emphasized at the expense of the "reality principle," the latter being the introjected representation of scarcity according to which "he who does not work—or follow the rules—shall not eat." Whereas conventional Americans are a country working hard to work its way out of poverty, the freaks are a rich country taking it easy. The white middle-class youth movement was in a profound sense "just for laughs," and any attempt to impose "seriousness" upon it was bound to negate its very reason for existence. As the (capital M) Movement became serious revolutionaries, the (small m) movement went to Woodstock.

The Woodstock Festival, held at Bethel, New York, August 18–21, 1969, was a symbolic event which crystallized the new culture phase. Perhaps 450,000 youths participated in the sensation of having, for three days, established a provisional Freak Utopia with untrammeled group solidarity, dope, sex, and music. By sheer weight of numbers official repression had been forestalled. This latter fact appeared to substantiate what became one of the hallmarks of the new phase, the neo-hippie notion that overt politics is superfluous since cultural and psychic changes will bring about the same result ("The revolution was yesterday. Where were you?"). The new phase gave impetus to the formation of rural communes, in which thousands of people engaged in building their own utopias. The needs of freak craftsmen and farmers were serviced by the *Whole Earth Catalog* ("Access to Tools"). The new phase also saw increased interest in organic foods and ecology. Campus disturbances and street violence, meanwhile, declined sharply. It is difficult to estimate how far the decline would have gone were it not for the federal government's prosecution of the Chicago Conspiracy Eight (later Seven).

The mood of the Woodstock-Aquarian Interlude was shattered by the invasion of Cambodia announced by President Nixon on April 30, 1970, and the subsequent massacre of four students by the Ohio National Guard at Kent State University (May 2). These events set off a campus general strike, with building seizures and suspension of classes at many schools. In retrospect, these events proved to be the Storm before the Calm.

While, as of 1971, the freak subculture continues to persist and even grow, the intense dissidence and sense of irreconcilable opposition are increasingly absent. In growing numbers freaks take to scrounging regular incomes, raising families, registering as Democrats, and setting up small businesses and cooperatives run either by single individuals ("hip capitalists") or "collectives." In many ways they are becoming assimilated to the traditional American pattern of the urban ethnic group. At the same time, many among them are being swept away into various movements of Consciousness Contraction, the forms of which are every bit as bizarre as were the forms of consciousness expansion. Inasmuch as the social order was not swiftly changed to suit the dictates of expanded freak-consciousness, and without any prospect of such a transformation in the offing, many youths seek devices that promise to liquidate this consciousness, now a painful burden. They turn to cults and practices that will impose severe external discipline upon them, subjecting them to the stern demands of absolute authority, and guaranteeing them mindless ecstasy.

One of the principal modes of consciousness contraction is the use of heroin, that old psychic painkiller of the black ghetto. As of 1971, heroin is fashionable among white middle-class youth the way that LSD was during the heyday of hippieism or that amphetamines were during the most conflicted period of the New New Left. There is no more absolute authority than that of heroin, since the addict's entire life revolves around the acquisition of the drug.

In terms of consciousness contraction, heroin's most prominent rival appears to be the Jesus Freak movement; and the dramatic suddenness with which addicts are converted and then reportedly led to kick their habits tends to indicate the functional interchangeability of heroin and Jesus. In any case, confused young people are being swept in growing numbers into sects of

ecstatic chiliastic fundamentalist Christianity and, under the guiding hand of authoritarian preachers, abandon drugs and sex and
become "high on Jesus."

The situation does not easily lend itself to optimism.

Midpendix

a scrapbook of consequences of and responses to Life in a Fake Universe. (or, can a young girl from a little mining town in the Contradictions of Capitalism find True Consciousness as the bride of a Global Village?)

"There are no truths outside the Gates of Eden"

I had come to rap about the revolution. Since the Fish have come to represent the quintessence of commitment in a rock group, I was searching for a few predictions, a reminiscence of life at the barricades [in Chicago], and perhaps a scenario or two. But Country Joe snickered. "There isn't going to be any revolution. Let's be realistic," he said, and went off to brush his teeth. . . .

"Why isn't there going to be a revolution?"

"Because you have to control things, and most of the people I know aren't ready for that. They want a leaderless society."

"What about the guerrillas?" I offered.

"I don't know any. I know a lot of people wearing Che Guevara teeshirts . . . what a bunch of tripped-out freaks. Three years ago, we were hoboes singing our hearts out about the virtues of the open road. Last year, we were Indians. Now, we're revolutionaries. Man, if the revolution ever comes for real, they'll probably use Andy Warhol munitions. You throw it and this big sign comes on —Pow!" . . .

Country Joe McDonald is half Jewish.

(Richard Goldstein in *The Village Voice,* October 4–10, 1968.)

It's all a myth, man. Yippie's a myth. The pig's a myth. I'm a myth; who ever heard of a commie-anarchist-terrorist with a color television?

—Abbie Hoffman

Learjet stereos go to sit-ins, love-ins, anywhere there's a demonstration. Thirty dollars. Turn one on.

—Radio commercial, late 1968

Other P.R. Agencies
Build Up the Establishment.
We Build Up the Anti-establishment.
News releases, press conferences, brochures, newsletters, flyers, publicity for demonstrations and rallies, articles in magazines and newspapers, your spokesmen on radio and television talk shows.
Advertising, graphic design, photography, fund raising, buttons et al.
Clients we've serviced: National Mobilization to End the War in Vietnam, National Conference for New Politics, Government of the Republic of Biafra, California Grape Pickers, N.Y. State Freedom and Peace Party, American Documentary Films, Parents Aid Society, the Guardian, the New York Free Press.
Michael C. Luckman
Public Relations Agency For the Movement
                                       —advertisement in the *Guardian*

In the name of the people of the City of Los Angeles, I order you to disperse!
We are the people! We *are* the people! WE ARE THE PEOPLE!
          (The final lines of "L.A.P.D.," by Ill Wind, on *Flashes,*
                              ABC Records, ABCS-641.)

[Connie Devanney, vocalist of Ill Wind] suggested doing a difficult number that hadn't quite jelled at rehearsals. Then [Ken Frankel, leader-songwriter of Ill Wind] exploded:
    "We're trying to sell records. We don't want to be avant-garde. We want to be rich."
                    (*New York Times Magazine,* September 29, 1968.)

If you won't listen to your parents, the Man or the Establishment . . . Why should you listen to us?
    (from a Columbia Records advertisement, September, 1968.)

Nothing is real, and nothing to get hung about. . . .
                (The Beatles "Strawberry Fields Forever," 1967.)

MOVEMENT: That's quite an emotional way of expressing themselves going into the streets on Election Day and you would agree
that not everybody would be expressing their total freedom by
doing that. There are alternatives . . .

JERRY: No, no. I think people are basically emotional and I think
that reason is used to give justification for fears. I don't think anybody intellectualizes himself into becoming a revolutionary. He
feels that he just absolutely needs to do this and the intellectualism
is most usually an excuse. Like I have a feeling that when people
go to demonstrations the demands that are made, the issues that
are raised are really irrelevant to why they came.

They're here because they want to pick up girls, they want to
have a good time, they want to be where the action is, they want
to fight the cops, they want to make history, they want to do something unusual. It's all personal and emotional reasons and then
you hear all the intellectualizations, the battle of the leaflets, and
man, there are a lot of crazy people here really acting on some
nutty levels . . . there's a leaflet about Marxism, who the hell
knows from his Marxism?

(Movement, November 1968.)

Community was built in many ways. For instance, pissing.
There we were, all crowded together, and no doors saying Men
and Ladies. You could go out to a tree, but it was really a hassle
to get through the people, especially if you were on the left bank
where you had to climb a rope down a wall to get out. One guy
who was on that side tells it like this: I had been there for hours
and I really had to piss something fierce. So this other guy says
well let's just do it right there pointing to a place where there
aren't any people standing. I said ok but when I got there I just
couldn't piss—guess I'm just hung up. So I walked a few feet
away and kind of turned my back and began to piss. About this
time a couple comes walking by and the guy notices me and says
"That's great, that's community, man!"

The Pentagon confrontation served to unify the Movement
in America many ways, and one of these was between the New
Left politicos and the hippies. For in the front lines holding off
the bayonets from the people behind were many long-haired flower
children, who talked to the troops and faced the gas and carried

water and food, and were in for the long haul. And among the SDS
contingent, we passed the hash pipe in full view of the troops, the
smoke from the dope mingling with the flaming draft cards. And
this form of rebellion was real, was not an internal isolationist
reaction, but an affirmation of our new community, and strength
and lack of fear.

(from coverage of the confrontation at the Pentagon,
October 21–22, 1967, in the *Washington Free Press,*
Pentagon Special Edition, Vol. II, No. 18.)

A whole generation of young people manifests a malaise, a
discontent. More than ever their lives are channelled. The students
know that their lives are on a one-way street to corrupt and
hedonistic suburbia, that their personal problems and hang-ups
are common to their peers—but they don't see politics as the answer to their problems. They've heard all the old radical arguments,
but people don't accept arguments just because they sound correct. They accept them when they see that the arguments make
sense OUT OF THEIR OWN LIVES. We argued that politics of
confrontation provides activity based on an elan and community
which shows young people that we CAN make a difference, we
CAN hope to change the system, and also that life within the radical movement can be liberated, fulfilling and meaningful—rather
than the plastic of suburbia or the tired intellectual arrogance of
the old left. . . .

. . . Most of us have been organizing for a long time. Like
that old leadership, we too believed our politics wasn't relevant to
people: Don't be too radical. It'll alienate people. Get 'em on
bread and butter issues. Bring 'em along slow. Build consciousness.

We were all breast-fed on the same milk.

Then Columbia happened and while our heads were still reel-
ing, we were in Chicago and the cops helped our heads "reel"
some more. Things were happening. Radical politics wasn't turning EVERYBODY off. Somebody was in those buildings. Somebody was in the streets of Chicago.

We began to feel, for the first time, that the situation was real.
Not tomorrow. Or the next year. But real. We began to feel that
our movement had something to offer to people: not just a rejec-

tion of plastic, cool-slick computerized America, but positive things: the way we lived in the buildings in Columbia, the way we developed community in Chicago's only more overt police state. A new culture, liberated, vibrant, audacious. A new style of activism—saying and doing who you really are. And now belief in yourself as a person really able to understand freedom, and to fight for it. (Bill Ayers, Jim Mellon, and Terry Robbins, leaders of the "Lurleen Wallace Memorial Caucus," a militant faction in the University of Michigan SDS Chapter, describing their ouster of a more moderate faction from control; "Ann Arbor SDS Splits," *New Left Notes,* November 11, 1968. The editors say that they printed the piece because "we see the situation at Ann Arbor as typical of many SDS chapters throughout the country.")

And the students? They, alas, are indeed for the most part rebels without a cause—and without a hope of accomplishing anything except mischief and ruin. . . .

My own view is that a significant minority of today's student body obviously consists of a mob who have no real interest in higher education or in the life of the mind, and whose passions are inflamed by a debased popular culture that prevails unchallenged on the campus. We are reluctant to believe this because so many of the young people who constitute this mob have high I.Q.'s, received good academic grades in high school, and because their popular culture is chic rather than philistine in an old-fashioned way. Which is to say: we are reluctant to believe that youngsters of a certain social class, assembled on the grounds of an educational institution, can be a "mob," in the authentic sociological sense of that term. We are also reluctant to believe it because many of these students are our children. . . .

(Irving Kristol, "A Different Way To Restructure the
University," *New York Times Magazine,*
December 8, 1968.)

. . . Action at the state of the university rally: There's another "state of the university" from the president's one. It's all of us being channelled by the "educational process" into straight ties and collars. Some of us to destroy young kids' minds in school.

Some of us to distort the truth in the media. Some of us to help murder Vietnamese, or "contain" blacks in their ghettos. Most of us simply to do the man's dirty work—while he lives off a Guatemalan's 90¢ a day labor. And—most important—there's still another state of the university: us refusing to buy their line, or be what they need us to be. Dancing in their corridors, screaming at their speeches, telling 'em we're hip to their lies.

(Ayers, et al., in *New Left Notes,* November 11, 1968.)

Beware of leaders, heroes, organizers: watch that stuff. Beware of structure-freaks. They do not understand.

We know The System doesn't work out because we're living in its ruins. We know that leaders don't work out because they have all led us only to the present, the good leaders equally with the bad. (Who caused more suffering, Hitler or St. Paul?) It doesn't matter whether the leader is good or bad: leading per se is bad. The medium is the message, and the message of leadership is Vietnam. Concentration camps. Riots on Haight Street.

What The System calls organization—linear organization—is a Systematic cage, arbitrarily limiting the possible. It's never worked before. It's always produced the present.

And heroes are only heroes, nothing more.

Any man who *wants* to lead you is The Man. Think: why would anyone *want* to lead *me?* Think: why should I pay for his trip? Think.

LBJ is Our Leader, and you know where that's at.

Watch out for cats who want to play The System's games, 'cause you can't beat The System at its own games, and you know that. Why should we trade one Establishment for another Establishment?

Do your thing. Be what you are. If you don't know what you are, find out.

Fuck leaders.

(*communications company,* San Francisco, April 6, 1967; reprinted in the *Seed,* Chicago, Vol I., No. 12, November 1967; anthologized in Jerry Hopkins, ed., *The Hippie Papers,* pp. 17–18.)

Maintain a sense of humor. People who take themselves too seriously are powercrazy. If they win, it will be haircuts for all. BEWARE OF POWER FREAKS.

> (Abbie Hoffman from *Revolution For the Hell of It,* publ. late 1968.)

. . . Action at the meeting: what the old leadership called "heckling"—but what was really people for the first time trying to question, to communicate openly, unhostilely, honestly.

> (Ayers, *et al.,* in *New Left Notes,* November 11, 1968.)

Bill Gerchow, New York, N.Y.: It's curious that your anti-electoral editorial (Oct. 26) reinforces a certain new left disposition. You should consider Lenin's instructive that "As long as you are unable to disperse the bourgeois parliament and every other type of reactionary institution, you must work inside them . . . ; otherwise you risk becoming mere babblers." This "legal" participation assists in organizing the masses and in stimulating among them a revolutionary mood. "Without a revolutionary mood among the masses, and without conditions favoring the growth of this mood, revolutionary tactics would never be converted into action. Expressing one's 'revolutionariness' solely by hurling abuse at parliamentary opportunism, solely by repudiating participation in parliaments, is very easy; but just because it is too easy, it is not the solution for a difficult, a very difficult problem."

But apparently nothing seems difficult to those who want to "make" a revolution "for the hell of it." Moreover, it's understandable why those with this pronounced "disorder" (and let it be said there are far worse maladies) are spending more and more time disrupting radical forums and meetings. The technique is called: Here We Are, Now What's All This Shit? As Engels said almost a hundred years ago, "What childish innocence it is to present impatience as a theoretically convincing argument!"

> (Letter to the *Guardian;* Correspondence, *Guardian,* November 30, 1968.)

MOVEMENT: What kinds of organizations come to mind? There's been a lot of talk about new forms of organization . . .

JERRY: The problem right now is not organization and I don't

think about that much. The problem is reaching people and whatever kind of organization is needed to do that is the right one. We
don't first have to think about how we make decisions or how we
control various groups; the main thing is to effect it. As the need
changes the form of organization I suppose will change.

Eventually there will be a greater need for secrecy, need for
going underground, a much greater togetherness. But it cannot be
invented out of thin air; and it can't be invented because Lenin did
it and therefore we should do it if we want to be like Lenin. It
can only be created when it is organic to our environment. Right
now it just isn't organic.

(Movement, November 1967.)

Like Hoffman, Jerry Rubin seeks violent encounters with
authority. With Rubin, though, there are no overtones of humor.
He is very serious, and it annoys Hoffman. At Chicago, they
weren't speaking. Hoffman puts down Rubin's "Marxist approach."

(The New York Times Magazine, September 15, 1968.)

We are "self-styled."   —SDS activist

A revolution for which one must suffer is a revolution of "papa."

The more I make love, the more I make revolution; the more I make revolution, the more I make love.
                    —French student slogans, May 1968

Notes

CHAPTER 2

1. Allen Woode, "How the Pentagon Learned to Stop Worrying and Love Peace Marchers," *Ramparts*, February 1968.

CHAPTER 3

1. Kenneth Keniston, *The Uncommitted* (New York: Dell, 1965), pp. 180–84. Paper.

2. *Ibid.*, pp. 184–87.

3. Phillip Altbach, "The Need for Leadership and Ideology," *New University Thought*, Autumn 1961.

4. "Port Huron Statement," printed as an SDS pamphlet in 1962.

5. Staughton Lynd, "The New Radicals and Participatory Democracy," *Dissent*, Summer 1965. Reprinted as a pamphlet by SDS.

6. Bertram D. Wolfe, *Three Who Made a Revolution* (5th ed.; Boston: Beacon Press, 1959). Paper.

7. "Extra Be-In" issue, *East Village Other*, April 1967.

8. Burton H. Wolfe, *The Hippies* (New York: New American Library, 1968), p. 178 ff. Paper.

9. Abbie Hoffman, "My Life to Live," *New York Free Press*, October 3, 1968.

CHAPTER 4

1. John K. Galbraith, *The New Industrial State* (Boston: Houghton Mifflin, 1967).

2. From a speech by Virgil E. Boyd, president of Chrysler Corporation, as quoted in *Newsweek,* July 1, 1968.

3. Michael Harrington, *The Accidental Century* (New York: Pelican, 1968), p. 84. Paper.

4. *Ibid.,* p. 108.

5. Tuli Kupferberg, "The Politics of Love," *East Village Other,* May 1–15, 1967.

6. Charles Giuliano, *Avatar,* August 2–15, 1968.

7. Karl Polanyi, *The Great Transformation* (Boston: Beacon Press, 1957), p. 256. Paper.

8. John Poppy, "New Era in Industry: It's Okay to Cry in the Office," *Look,* July 8, 1968.

9. *Ibid.*

10. *Ibid.*

11. *Ibid.*

12. *Ibid.*

13. *Ibid.*

14. *Ibid.*

15. *Ibid.*

16. *Ibid.*

17. *Ibid.*

18. *Ibid.*

19. *Ibid.*

20. Herbert Marcuse, *One Dimensional Man* (9th ed.; Boston: Beacon Press, 1968), p. 255. Paper.

CHAPTER 5

1. Galbraith, *op. cit.,* pp. 294–295.

2. *Ibid.,* p. 380.

3. Marcuse, *op. cit.,* pp. 7, 18.

4. *Ibid.,* pp. 254–256.

5. Allen Graubard, "Herbert Marcuse—One-Dimensional Pessimism," *Dissent,* May-June, 1968.

6. Marcuse, *op. cit.,* p. 250.

7. *Ibid.,* pp. 256–257.

8. Arlene E. Bergman, "All the Rules Broken," *New Left Notes,* July 8, 1968.

9. Marcuse, *op. cit.,* p. 257.

CHAPTER 6

1. Harvey Cox, *Playboy,* January 1968.

2. Bob Dylan, "Ballad of a Thin Man," *Highway 61 Revisited,* Columbia CL 2389.

3. Sanche de Gramonts, "A Bas—Everything," *New York Times Magazine,* June 2, 1968.

4. Jefferson Airplane, "D.C.B.A.-25," *Surrealistic Pillow,* RCA-Victor LSP 3766.

5. Joel Fort, "The AMA Lies About Pot," *Ramparts,* August 24, 1968.
6. *Medical World News,* April 23, 1965, p. 62.
7. *Ibid.,* p. 71.
8. *Medical World News,* October 14, 1966, pp. 68–69.

CHAPTER 7

1. John Hersey, *The Algiers Motel Incident* (New York: Bantam Books, 1968), p. 59. Paper.
2. Jean Bloch-Michel, "France—A New Kind of Rebellion," *Dissent,* July–August 1968.
3. Headline, *Los Angeles Free Press,* October 6–12, 1967.

CHAPTER 8

1. *Look,* August 20, 1968.
2. *Ibid.*
3. Letters to the Editor, *East Village Other,* August 1–15, 1967.

CHAPTER 9

1. Bob Dylan, "My Back Page," *Another Side of Bob Dylan,* Columbia CL-2193, 1964.
2. Bertram D. Wolfe, *The Hippies,* p. 110.
3. James J. Carey, *The College Drug-Scene* (Cliffside, N.J.: Prentice-Hall, 1968), p. 166. This individual is described by the author as a "21-year-old part-time carpenter."
4. Wolfe, *op. cit.,* pp. 168–169.
5. Carey, *op. cit.,* p. 167. Again, the young Bay Area part-time carpenter.

CHAPTER 10

1. William H. Grier and Price M. Cobbs, *Black Rage* (New York: Bantam Books, 1968), p. 58. Paper.
2. Cf. Marvin Garson's description of the participants in recent Berkeley street-freak riots:

> They believed in a different form of organization, suggested in the strange phrase "affinity groups." You get together with people you understand, whose heads are in the same place as yours: a family of sorts; you become a tight-knit, functional working unit with a speciality of your own, something you do well; and then you go out and do it. *Village Voice,* July 11, 1968.

3. Patrick Seale and Maureen McConville, *Red Flag, Black Flag: French Revolution,* (New York: Ballantine Books, 1968), p. 37. Paper.
4. Jerry Densch, "Haight Street Blues," *The Movement,* September 1968.
5. See Kenneth Keniston, *Young Radicals,* (New York: Harvest Books), pp. 160–173, for a dramatic instance of this.

6. Letter to campus organizers from National SDS, February 6, 1967.

7. From "In White America," speech at an SDS-sponsored conference at Princeton University, February 17–19, 1967; reprinted in *Guardian*, March, 1967.

8. *New Left Notes*, November 11, 1968.

9. Cf. the remarks of Abbie Hoffman, a systematic freak-radical theorist, in the article "My Life to Live," *New York Free Press*, October 3, 1968, and his recent book, *Revolution for the Hell of It* (New York: Dial Press, 1968).